PRAISE FOR *DARE TO W*

T0348985

"Chantal is a proven champion. Through perseverance, hard work, and inspiring leadership, she willed a chronically underperforming team of young women into national champions. Her winning approach extends beyond the court and can drive success in any setting."

—DR. RICHARD PEDDIE, Former President and CEO, Maple Leaf Sports & Entertainment

"Not only is Chantal Vallée a decorated basketball coach but also a championship teammate. As my partner in the broadcast booth, Chantal brought the same kind of leadership traits to our entire production crew and illustrated how and why there's been buy-in from her Windsor teams that won five straight national titles. Chantal's commitment to leadership has been integral to winning on and off the floor."

—ARASH MADANI, National Reporter, Sportsnet

"Chantal has this basketball set play she runs in practice. She is the one in, bounding the ball to a designated player; only when she initiates the play, she purposefully throws the ball to a non-designated player. At that moment, the playbook is discarded and innovation begins. Her players know X's and O's are the kiss of death without daring to adapt. Read on, and you will never be caught off guard again."

—RON MACLEAN, Host of *Hockey Night in Canada*

"Chantal personifies all qualities of an outstanding leader. Understanding leadership theories is only one part of the equation. Her execution and the trust of her players in both difficult and contentious times lead to the ultimate success. This book definitely gives the blueprint for winning in sports, business, and life in general."

—PAUL JONES, Sportscaster, NBA TV Canada

"*Dare to Win* is a masterclass in leadership and what it takes to win, whether that's in sports or business. With a blend of practical strategies, academic insights, and stories from the incredible U of Windsor journey to unparalleled success, Chantal Vallée and Gordon Bloom provide a playbook for anyone striving to build a culture of excellence. Whether you're a coach, business leader, or someone seeking a roadmap to do the seemingly impossible, this book will ignite your vision and equip you with practical tools to overcome the odds and achieve greatness."

—MANO WATSA, President, Point Guard College

"*Dare to Win* is a must-read for leaders on the court and in the boardroom. As the lines between the worlds of sport, business, and entertainment continue to blur, so too are the skill sets shared by championship-winning teams and successful businesses. Vallée and Dr. Bloom have drawn up a game-winning play for coaches and entrepreneurs alike."

—LAURA CORRENTI, Founder & CEO,
Deep Blue Sports + Entertainment

"Chantal is one of the brightest minds and best coaches I've had the privilege of working with. Her success is a direct result of the well-rounded coaching philosophy along with the attention to detail she brings in all facets. *Dare to Win* is not only a great book for other coaches to read, but it provides a unique insight into how to build a top tier program no matter what sport, business, or organization."

—RYAN SCHMIDT, Assistant Coach, Atlanta Hawks, NBA

"Coach Vallée's book is one of the most interesting books on the subject of coaching and leadership that I have read. It is a combination lecture series and novel. Most books like this lack such continuity. This book will often challenge you to evaluate what you just read and make an assessment. You will become a better student of the coach and leader game and will, no doubt, make some adjustments to your approach in the next season, or the rest of this current one."

—DEL HARRIS, Vice President of the Texas Legends, NBA G-League,
Former NBA Head Coach of the Rockets, Bucks, and Lakers

"Coach Vallee's personal leadership journey is fascinating as she learned to marry academic research with personal ambition, operational process, personal experience, expert mentorship, and personal grit to create a culture and habit of winning. Chantal shares many processes, tools, and mindsets that others can use in their own quests to win. Her demonstration of a key leadership role being to protect her team from outside pressures is an example that all aspiring leaders need to take special note of. I will

certainly make it my practice to recommend this book to aspiring and accomplished leaders, as is my habit when I come across a great book."
—ALLAN CONWAY DBA, Former Dean and Professor Emeritus, Strategy & Entrepreneurship, Odette School of Business

"A wonderful partnership between a practitioner and a scientist, capturing the intricacies of the many processes and practices involved in "daring to win." In a refreshingly candid way, Coach Vallée and Professor Bloom offer brilliant insights into building and leading high-performance championship teams. This book shows both why and how to do it. Read it and reflect on its wisdom."
—DR. SOPHIA JOWETT, Department of Psychology, Loughborough University

"*Dare to Win* is a unique combination of proven championship coaching lessons with insights from decades of research. Vallée and Bloom combine their unique world-class talents from the court and the classroom to provide coaches with a rare glimpse into what it takes to build a winning program. I have no doubt this book will become a trusted resource for coaches of any sport willing to invest in building better programs and better people."
—DR. WADE GILBERT, Coaching Scientist, Author, Award-winning Professor, Department of Kinesiology, California State University

"Congratulations to Chantal and Gordon for sharing their numerous insights into the world of elite sports coaching and leadership. This is a valuable resource for coaches, managers, and administrators in sport and other contexts who seek to shape environments that enable thriving for all actors."
—DR. CLIFF MALLETT, OAM, Former Olypmpic & World Championship-Winning Coach

"*Dare to Win* provides compelling, evidence-based, practical ideas to develop, implement, and sustain successfully high-performance programs. I highly recommend it to all coaches and sports administrators."
—DR. KOH KOON TECH, FIBA Instructor & Basketball Coach, Secretary General, Southeast Asia Basketball Association

"This book is about much more than basketball. Vallée and Bloom outline the many challenges of coaching and leadership and provide actual examples and antidotes based on Coach Vallée's championship-building journey. A highly recommended read for leaders in all walks of life."

—PETER SMITH, Former Ice Hockey Coach,
Team Canada & McGill Martlets

"A great new resource that shows the value of how research-based practice can influence successful coaches—and vice versa. This gives coaches the opportunity to reflect on their performance environment at any level of competition and shows how great partnerships in coaching and academia can advance the profession of coaching. Examples of thoughtful leaders in action."

—CHRISTINE BOLGER, Associate Director of Coach Education,
United States Olympic & Paralympic Committee

"This work explores the positive impact of great coaching on athletes' physical and mental growth, but, importantly, emphasizes healthy character and social development needed for humans who work in complex, competitive, and ever-changing environments. These ideas must be incorporated into our player and coaching development pathways at every level of hockey and sport."

—KATHERINE HENDERSON, President & CEO, Hockey Canada

DARE TO WIN

The Blueprint to Building and Leading
High-Performance and Championship Teams

Chantal N. Vallée, MA,
5-Time National Champion Coach

Gordon A. Bloom, PhD
World Renowned Coaching Leadership
Researcher and Practitioner

Copyright © Chantal Vallée and Gordon Bloom, 2025

Published by ECW Press
665 Gerrard Street East
Toronto, Ontario, Canada M4M 1Y2
416-694-3348 / info@ecwpress.com

All rights reserved. No part of this publication may be reproduced,
stored in a retrieval system, or transmitted in any form by any
process — electronic, mechanical, photocopying, recording,
or otherwise — without the prior written permission of the
copyright owners and ECW Press. The scanning, uploading, and
distribution of this book via the internet or via any other means
without the permission of the publisher is illegal and punishable
by law. This book may not be used for text and data mining, AI
training, and similar technologies. Please purchase only authorized
electronic editions, and do not participate in or encourage
electronic piracy of copyrighted materials. Your support of the
authors' rights is appreciated.

Editors for the Press: Michael Holmes & Jennifer Smith
Copy editor: Crissy Boylan
Cover design: Jessica Albert

LIBRARY AND ARCHIVES CANADA CATALOGUING
IN PUBLICATION

Title: Dare to win : the blueprint to building and leading
high performance and championship teams / Chantal N.
Vallée, MA and Gordon A. Bloom, PhD.

Names: Vallée, Chantal N., author. | Bloom, Gordon A.,
author.

Description: Includes bibliographical references.

Identifiers: Canadiana (print) 20240525701 | Canadiana
(ebook) 20240528409

ISBN 978-1-77041-825-7 (softcover)
ISBN 978-1-77852-384-7 (PDF)
ISBN 978-1-77852-383-0 (ePub)

Subjects: LCSH: Leadership. | LCSH: Coaching (Athletics)

Classification: LCC BF637.L4 V35 2025 | DDC 158/.4—dc23

This book is funded in part by the Government of Canada. *Ce livre est financé en partie par le gouvernement du Canada.* We also
acknowledge the support of the Government of Ontario through the Ontario Book Publishing Tax Credit, and through
Ontario Creates.

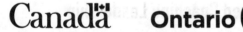

PRINTED AND BOUND IN CANADA   PRINTING: MARQUIS   5   4   3   2   1

Purchase the print edition and receive the ebook free.
For details, go to ecwpress.com/ebook.

This book is printed on Sustana EnviroBook™, a recycled
paper, and other controlled sources that are certified by the
Forest Stewardship Council®.

ECW Press is a proudly independent, Canadian-owned
book publisher. Find out how we make our books better
at ecwpress.com/about-our-books

This book is dedicated to all those who stand at the edge,
uncertain and afraid to take the first step—
may you find the courage to leap, for the unknown holds
endless possibilities, and a full life of beauty.

"It is not because things are difficult that we do not dare, it is because we do not dare that they are difficult."

—SENECA

CONTENTS

NOTE FROM CHANTAL

I am delighted to share the knowledge and strategies that transformed the University of Windsor women's basketball team from worst to first. My path began during my years as a graduate student at McGill University, where I immersed myself in the study of leadership and coaching success under the guidance of Dr. Gordon Bloom. It was then that I realized a gap existed between theory and practice in coaching.

The world's best researchers were not professional coaches, and the top coaches in the world were not scholars. The challenge lay in applying scientifically proven leadership theories in a practical coaching setting. I was fortunate to bridge this gap, becoming a researcher who directly applied her findings in the coaching field to achieve success.

The blueprint for this success is what I am sharing with you in this book. The book is divided into four quarters, mirroring the timeline of a basketball game. I encourage you to keep a journal nearby, as exercises and reflective practices are suggested at the end of each quarter; you can apply these principles to your own program, business, or life.

Throughout the book, you will encounter time-out boxes, mimicking those of a game, with a deeper probe into the academic research. These research insights, carefully curated with the collaboration of Dr. Bloom, form the foundation of my coaching and leadership philosophy. I have also included inspiring stories, anecdotes, and concepts that have contributed to my success along the way. Leadership knows no boundaries and transcends all disciplines and crafts. My goal is for this book to equip you with the tools and mindset to achieve remarkable success in your own life. Together, let's embark on this transformative journey.

WINDSOR LANCERS STATS (1968–2005)

- Regular season: 154–314 (0.329)
- Playoffs: 8–13 (0.380)
- Overall: 190–406 (0.319)

CHANTAL VALLÉE'S COACHING RECORD

WINDSOR LANCERS STATS (2005–PRESENT)

- Regular season: 277–97 (0.741)
- Playoffs: 49–13 (0.790)
- Overall: 416–152 (0.732)

- Conference titles: 10
- Provincial championships: 6
- National championships: 5

Player development:

- Professional players: 7
- Olympians: 1

HAMILTON HONEY BADGERS STATS (2018–2019)

- Regular season: 10–10 (0.500)
- Playoffs: 1–1 (0.500)
- Overall: 11–11 (0.500)

Notable achievements in the franchise's first season:

- Qualified for the league's final four tournament
- Upset No. 1 seed in playoff semi-finals
- Lost in the league final to finish second overall

NOTE FROM GORDON

The remarkable people who have left an indelible mark in university sports can amaze and inspire. Coaches like Pat Summitt, John Wooden, and Anson Dorrance all have had unscientific accounts written of their careers, which have helped broaden our understanding of the profound wisdom, behaviours, and strategies that propelled them to unparalleled success. Summitt's athlete-centred style, based on commitments to effective communication and attentive listening, propelled her to eight National Collegiate Athletic Association (NCAA) basketball titles. Wooden's meticulous disciplinary methods and his planning and teaching skills earned him ten NCAA championships. Dorrance's 22 NCAA soccer championships showcased his ability to push his players to their very limits while cultivating an environment that fostered unity and camaraderie.

In the midst of these celebrated coaches, Coach Vallée emerges as an extraordinary figure. As we dive into her journey, we discover a unique trait that sets her apart. Unlike her peers, Vallée grounded her coaching philosophy in published coaching research, drawing inspiration from her own master's thesis. This distinction grants us unprecedented access to the inner workings of her mind, uncovering the secrets behind her thriving program. Despite an increased number of publications on coaching science around the world, there is limited scientific evidence on how coaches develop and maintain programs that achieve continuous success. This book is a treasure trove that our scientific realm has been longing for.

The impact of this book extends far beyond the realm of sports. Its principles find resonance in diverse domains, including the business world. For just as building and upholding a culture of excellence in a university team parallels the challenges faced by companies, so, too, does this book offer universal lessons in the pursuit of greatness.

It has been an honour and pleasure working with Chantal on this project, which has brought together our 20 years of collaborative work.

FOREWORD

Success in sports, as in life, is about far more than winning games—it's about building something enduring, inspiring others to rise to their potential, and creating a legacy that outlasts your time on the court. That's why I'm so honoured to write the foreword for *Dare to Win*. This book isn't just a chronicle of championships; it's a masterclass in leadership, resilience, and the art of turning vision into reality.

Chantal Vallée has long been a name I've admired in the world of basketball. From the first time we met while she was coaching professional men and building the Canadian Elite Basketball League, I felt an instant connection to her story. It reminded me of my own early days coaching professional men all over the world. Whether it was the British Basketball League or the NBA Development League, we both know the unique challenges—and opportunities—that come with working in start-up environments and building something from the ground up. Those experiences taught me invaluable lessons about leadership, innovation, and perseverance—lessons that resonate throughout *Dare to Win*.

Chantal's journey with the University of Windsor women's basketball team is nothing short of extraordinary. Transforming a last-place program into a five-time national championship powerhouse required vision, grit, and an unwavering belief in her players. As someone who has won championships at multiple levels, including leading the Toronto Raptors to their historic 2019 NBA Championship, I can confidently say that the blueprint she shares in this book is exactly the kind of formula for success I've followed throughout my career.

What makes *Dare to Win* so impactful is its fusion of academic insight and real-world application. Chantal and Dr. Gordon Bloom have crafted a guide that bridges the gap between theory and practice. Their scientifically proven leadership strategies mirror my own approach to building winning teams, whether it's cultivating a culture of excellence, fostering deep connections with players, or empowering individuals to rise to their fullest potential. My academic journey, earning a PhD in sports leadership from Concordia University Chicago, focused on the impact of charitable giving foundations of professional athletes in their local communities. Through my research, I've come to understand the transformative power of leadership that goes beyond the court. It's about empathy, connection, and leaving a legacy that uplifts others. These same principles are at the heart of *Dare to Win*.

Chantal's ability to blend her academic background, coaching expertise, and visionary leadership is what makes this book so unique. She has lived the lessons she teaches, and her story proves that transformative leadership is not just possible—it's replicable.

Reading *Dare to Win* is like having a one-on-one with one of the most innovative minds in sports today. Whether you're a coach, entrepreneur, or leader in any field, you'll find actionable strategies and profound insights that will inspire you to rethink what's possible in your journey.

To Chantal: thank you for sharing your story and for creating a guide that will elevate leaders everywhere. To the readers: prepare to be inspired— you're about to gain the tools to create your own championship legacy.

Nick Nurse, PhD
Head Coach, Philadelphia 76ers
2019 NBA Champion Coach
2020 NBA Coach of the Year

PRE-GAME

P *rofessional suicide.* Those disturbing words, spoken by a colleague, echoed in my ears as I dared to entertain the idea of accepting the head coaching position of the University of Windsor Lancers women's basketball team back in 2005. The team's poor record and bottom-of-the-rankings status in Canada spoke volumes about their struggles. Throughout their nearly 50-year history, they had managed a grim four winning seasons. In the preceding two years, the Lancers had played over 60 matches, scraping together eight victories. The media cast them aside as nothing more than a stepping stone for their opponents. If I was to accept the job, I was slated to be their third head coach in as many years.

Windsor's proximity to the much-maligned American city of Detroit had unfairly tarnished its reputation. This perception, although unfounded, made it difficult to recruit players from outside the area. In fact, even the best local athletes were routinely seduced by the NCAA, the American university system, which provided full athletic scholarships—an advantage Windsor couldn't match. The mass exodus of Windsor's finest athletic talent had been a trademark of the city for decades. The Lancers were overlooked by everyone.

As a young coach on the cusp of a promising future, I sought advice from mentors and seasoned colleagues. Their unanimous counsel urged me to turn down the position. Despite interviewing for several other coaching jobs nationwide, only Windsor had extended an offer. With no other options, I half-heartedly accepted the job.

As I stepped in the program, the reality struck me harder than I had anticipated. Compounding the challenges I had anticipated was the program's heavy reliance on fundraising, a disheartening task considering the crippling economic crisis that had befallen the city. It was the fall of 2005, and the local economy, dependent on the struggling automotive industry, was crumbling. Unemployment rates soared to unprecedented heights, surpassing 15 percent. Foreclosure signs decorated the streets as families lost their homes. Desperation prompted many to leave Windsor in search of employment elsewhere. Recruiting top players to a city burdened with such hardships proved to be an uphill battle. Behind the closed doors of the gym, the state of the Lancers women's basketball team was also alarming. The players were unfamiliar with the demands of training at an advanced and competitive level, and their physical conditioning was lacking. The temptation to pack my bags and leave town was undeniable, but truthfully I had nowhere else to go. The Lancers were my sole source of income.

I sat in silence often, contemplating if I was more irritated at those who'd suggested this was a good idea or mad at myself for having believed I could possibly transform the Lancers' program. Amid moments of uncertainty, I did what I knew how to do: I shifted my perspective. From the reality before me, I envisioned a brighter future. Rather than questioning my decision to take the Windsor job, I focused on slowing down my thoughts, breathing deeply, and reassuring myself that everything would be all right. Through reading, journaling, drawing, and prayer, I found comfort and clarity. Those moments of mindfulness were transformative, as I began to imagine what this program *could* become, and what I wanted it for it: a national championship. I mentally rehearsed how I would respond to media questions about our success, visualized and felt the joy of winning, and even pictured the headlines and images of our triumphant team lifting up the trophy. Little did I know that these mindful practices would not only uplift my spirit but later uplift my entire team.

It was in one of my meditative sessions that I recalled the inspirational story of Gary Barnett, head coach of Northwestern University's NCAA Division 1 football team. In his book, *High Hopes: Taking the Purple to Pasadena*, Coach Barnett recounts announcing at his first press conference that he was going to take the Wildcats to the Rose Bowl. The crowd chuckled since the team was nearly always ranked last in their league; in fact, the school once set a record of 49 consecutive losses. His conviction, however, was strong, and his vision was clear: he expected victory. Coach Barnett reached his goal with this seemingly hopeless football program in under five years. Remembering his story made me more audacious: why not take the Lancers women's basketball program from the bottom of the Canadian university league all the way to a national championship? This became my vision. I didn't know exactly how I would achieve it, but in my mind I deeply committed to the intention. What started with a simple desire turned into a plan and then, six years later, into a tangible reality.

In March 2011, the Lancers became national champions for the first time in history. From that point forward, momentum propelled the program to win an unprecedented streak of five consecutive national titles. Seven players went on to play professionally, and one became an Olympian. The Windsor Lancers now hold the record for the most consecutive national championship wins for women's basketball in the country. Canada's national newspaper, *The Globe and Mail*, featured a cover story on the team with the headline "Coach Takes the Team from Outhouse to Penthouse."

FIRST QUARTER

The Vision

"I am enough of an artist to draw freely upon my imagination. Imagination is more important than knowledge. Knowledge is limited. Imagination encircles the world."

—ALBERT EINSTEIN

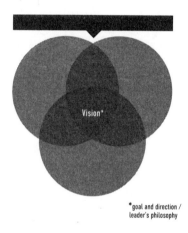

*goal and direction /
leader's philosophy

I n old French, the word *imaginer* meant sculpting, carving, or painting, suggesting that imagining is a creative process that results in a physical creation from a mental picture. Successful trailblazers use their imaginations to envision what they want to achieve without any restrictions, limiting factors, or obstacles hindering their access to resources. Visionaries are those who set a clear vision by imagining and generating ideas or concepts not yet realized. Much like artists, they leave many people wondering, "How did they do that?"

Our research clearly identified *vision* as the central piece of any successful endeavour. Leaders stepping into new roles do not rely on spur-of-the-moment decisions; they have a clear vision of what the future will look like before they even begin.

CHAPTER 1

Unleashing the Power of Vision

"Everything you can imagine is real."

—ATTRIBUTED TO PABLO PICASSO

A JOURNEY OF VISION

Six years before I arrived in Windsor as the new head coach, I was embarking a new chapter in my life in Montreal, Quebec, in the fall of 1999. McGill University, renowned for its academic distinction, became my home as I dove into the study of leadership and coaching science as a master's student. I was driven by the desire to become an extraordinary coach—one who would win championships. I didn't want to just give this profession "a try" or "my best shot." I would watch coaches winning on television and imagine myself in their places. Little did I know then, this steadfast intention marked the birth of my own coaching vision.

My initial year of graduate school revolved around course work that laid the foundation for my quest to uncover the secrets of successful coaches and leaders. As fate would have it, in my second year, McGill welcomed Dr. Gordon Bloom, an expert researcher in leadership success and coaching psychology. Was it mere coincidence, or had the power of my intention played a role in his arrival? Our connection was instantaneous, and I became Dr. Bloom's inaugural master's student at McGill. Under his direction, I read hundreds of books and research articles on leadership in the fields of entertainment, business, military, education, health care, and, of course, sports. From there, I landed on my specific research topic: how expert coaches transform bottom-ranking teams into perennial national champions.

The next step was my master's thesis project. I travelled across the country to interview team-sport coaches at the top of their games in university athletics. I remember visiting their state-of-the-art gyms, sitting in their comfortable offices, feeling rather intimidated. And yet these coaches couldn't have been more forthcoming or generous with their time. What amazed me was the remarkable consistency and synchronicity in their messages. While they were unaware of who else I was interviewing, or what questions I would pose, their answers revealed a wealth of recurring themes. Their coaching strategies and life lessons held a shared narrative.

As I analyzed the results, four key aspects of coaching excellence emerged. And at the heart of it all? Vision. All the coaches possessed a long-term plan for their programs, either crafted before taking the helm or shortly after. They recognized the need for transformative change to the status quo inherited from their predecessor. The catalyst for transformation was their ability to foster unwavering belief and inspire commitment in their athletes around this shared vision. Figure 1 shows the summary of my published findings, upon which this book is based.

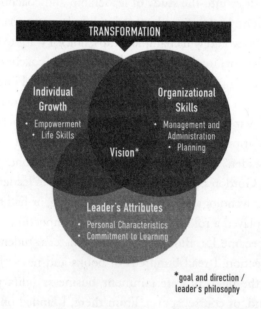

Figure 1: Coaching Success Model for Transforming a Program

This model of coaching success revealed that four characteristics bred a championship team: The leader's attributes category indicated their ability to display favourable behaviours in stressful situations. Individual growth described the coach's philosophy for their athletes' personal development. Organizational skills referred to the coach's vast number of responsibilities in all facets of their job. Lastly, the vision referred to the thoughts, ideas, and beliefs that the coach held with respect to creating a culture of excellence, and it focused on athletes buying into their vision.

The completion of my master's degree marked a pivotal moment of clarity in my journey to success. A vision, whether consciously pursued or silently harboured, has the power to shape our reality. Not only did my interviews with coaches emphasize the significance of vision, but it also emerged as the unifying thread in all the success stories of leadership I had explored. The findings of my research highlighted the immense power of a focused vision. Reflecting on my own life experiences, I recognized pivotal turning points when I had personally experienced or seen in others the spark of a desire become a thought, a vision, and eventually a fleshed-out journey to success.

THE POWER OF IMAGINATION

One of those significant turning points in my life traces back to 1984, when I was a young child. That summer, Sylvie Bernier made history by becoming the first female diver to secure an Olympic gold medal for Canada. As the three-metre springboard event in Los Angeles unfolded, all eyes, including my father's, were fixed on television screens. While many spectators expected a fierce competition between American and Chinese divers, what they didn't know was that Bernier had quietly shifted her approach. In the weeks leading up to the Olympics, she immersed herself in continuous visualization. Night after night, in the comfort of her home, she mentally rehearsed her dives, envisioning flawless execution and standing triumphantly atop the podium, to the point of joyful tears. Against all odds, Bernier astounded the world with her performance, clinching the gold medal. It was a groundbreaking moment for Canada, marking the country's first-ever gold medal in women's diving. I recall the impact this had on my father, who said to me, "Chantal, our minds are more powerful than we know. By imagining, we can manifest anything we want." Little did he know that his guidance would propel me far beyond his expectations. Soon after, I found myself dreaming of winning gold medals and being at the Olympics.

All of those dreams ended up materializing in their own way. My path intersected with Sylvie Bernier's when I served as a television analyst at the 2016 Rio Olympics. The Canadian Broadcasting Corporation asked us to collaborate on a radio show on the topic of winning. I was in awe as I listened to the story of her gold medal straight from the champion herself. The similarities to my thesis findings were staggering. She explained that the practice of using imagery wasn't popular in the early 1980s, but it was her path to realizing her dream of winning it all. She went as far as flying to Los Angeles to see the competition venue as it was being built. She asked where the diving board would be, analyzed where the sun rose and set, and inquired about the pool dimensions, change rooms, and podium. She even asked what kind of flowers would be presented to the winner. She came back to Montreal and trained, imagining that pool, the sun, the crowd, the flowers, and being crowned champion. One night, she found herself visualizing her win so intensely that she had tears running down her cheeks. It felt completely real. When the moment finally came for her to accept her gold medal, she was not overly emotional because her mind had already experienced the euphoria of victory. She had manifested this dream into reality weeks before stepping onto the Olympic stage.

From a wide-eyed young girl staring at my television, watching my hero on top of the podium, to a master's student, knee-deep in research, it always came back to the same thing: visions have power. When I accepted the job in Windsor six years after I started my master's, it was time to create my own coaching vision.

TIME-OUT

Imagery can be a complex concept as it includes all the senses, as opposed to simply visualizing, and can evoke intense emotions. Some view it as the creation or recreation of an experience that is etched in someone's mind. Traditionally, imagery is practised separately from physical activity and requires a calm, relaxed physical and mental state, so the imaginer can become fully engrossed in the imagery.[1] Research shows that successful athletes, coaches, and sport psychology practitioners alike have used imagery as an effective performance enhancing tool.[2]

CHAPTER 2

The First Season

"The beginning is the most important part of the work."
—PLATO

Upon my arrival in Windsor, there were only eight weeks before the team would arrive for our first practice. As I had not yet found a place to live, I opted to stay on campus in the vacant student residences for the summer months, and I used my evenings and weekends to look for an apartment to rent. I had to recruit a few last-minute players, fully move from Montreal to Windsor, and learn to work in a language that I had not yet mastered. It was a daunting task. Any free time I had before the season began was spent getting familiar with the players, the community, and the alumni. While the image of turning this team into national champions was always with me, instead of focusing on creating and writing a coaching vision, I got caught up in day-to-day operations.

My memory of my first day on campus remains vivid. First, I was unprepared in the wardrobe department: I had no Lancer-branded clothes, so I ventured out to the campus bookstore to outfit myself. Then having secured the keys to my office, I arrived to discover that there was no chair. When I inquired about one, I was told I had to go buy one myself. So, I found an old wooden elementary school chair in a dusty closet of the gym and used that for a long time. The red carpet certainly hadn't been rolled out.

My next experience was one that I hadn't quite anticipated. I had just turned 30, and my youth wasn't necessarily seen as an asset. When the captain of the team walked me around campus to introduce me, people thought I was the newest player. Even when my captain made a point to say that I was her new coach, they would still ask what position I played. I found myself repeatedly explaining and defending my position as the head coach. Looking back, it's a comical memory—how youthfully innocent I must have appeared! The truth is it was quite bothersome to me. Before the season started, I was determined to make a clear statement about my role, so I acquired suits, fancy shoes, and makeup for game day attire.

As we arrived at McMaster University for our first away game, I took the initiative and led the way off the bus in my tracksuit and running shoes and into the gym. The game day manager spotted me and introduced himself, graciously handing me the key to the players' locker room, since as a player I would need a spot to "get changed." I flipped the key to my captain and went to the main women's change room, where I would initiate my grand "physical transformation" into head coach. I swapped my tracksuit for a business professional look, unleashed my ponytail, tamed my hair, and even dared to apply makeup. But the pièce de résistance? Oh yes, high heels. Those devilish shoes were anything but comfortable. I wasn't accustomed to heels, but I was determined to exude professionalism and maturity. With squared shoulders and head held high, I marched confidently courtside. Just before tip-off, the referees walked over to the bench to greet the coaches, as is customary; they completely bypassed me and engaged instead with my male assistant. By the end of the game, we were down by 30 points. Finding respect or recognition in any form seemed like an uphill battle.

My first-ever home game was also quite an ordeal. I got my hair and makeup done, put on the best suit I had, and showed up to the gym confident that everyone would know I was the coach. And they probably did—but only because the sparse dozen or so fans who showed up were the parents and friends of the players. We lost the game—by a lot. I don't remember by exactly how much, but it was enough that I felt a sinking sense of embarrassment in the pit of my stomach. To compound matters, I decided to stick around and watch the men's game that followed. The hundreds and hundreds of fans flocking in made me feel even more embarrassed. Clearly our squad was not a draw. During the men's game, I closed my eyes and listened to the fans, imagining that their cheering was for us, visualizing a few years from now when we would be national champions. From that day forward, during the warm-up of every game, I gazed up at the empty 2,500-seat bleachers and told my assistant coach Tom, "One day this will be packed."

The quest for respect proved to be a multifaceted challenge. In that initial year, I found myself at the helm of a team of skeptical players. Not only was I a young and new coach, but English wasn't my first language. While my grasp of English was decent, it wasn't exactly top-notch. Speaking in front of a large group with energy and authority often led to comical linguistic tumbles. I distinctly remember shouting to my players on the court to "roll the ball" on offence, which was a direct translation from French. I meant for them to move the ball from one side of the court to the other. I repeated this phrase countless times until one player finally grew exasperated and actually did it. It was certainly a peculiar moment. On another occasion, the unintentional humour was untimely. I was displeased with the team's behaviour and decided to impose a curfew. I sternly demanded that everyone be in bed by 10 p.m., and if I heard of anyone "getting in late," they would face suspension. In my French accent, it turns out that "getting in late" sounded like "getting laid." Under different circumstances, it might have evoked laughter, but in this context, players were quite offended. If I had already established rapport with the team, such a blunder would have been comical, but with this group, frustration quickly mounted.

My coaching dynamic with the team was strained at best. I struggled to establish a new normal. Some players were constantly late to practice, and others did not give their all. Some gave me attitude, talked back, rolled their eyes, or did the opposite of what I asked. I tried to establish a program of healthy habits, encouraging them to rest and take naps, especially when on the road. Instead, a player complained that I, too, wasn't taking a nap. My assistants and I had to constantly police them, and it was exhausting. "We're going to lose anyway," one player said. I wanted to break the cycle of complacency, but a culture of defeat seemed deeply ingrained in the program.

We ended that first year with a record of nine wins and 13 losses. It was a difficult season and a steep learning curve for me. As a new coach, I ended the season overwhelmed and consumed by the demands of the job. I was working over 100 hours a week, feeling lost and verging on burnout. I realized that I had no clue what I had gotten myself into. Though I had heard the expert coaches talk about it in my master's interviews, I had not quite grasped how coaching went far beyond mere *X*s and *O*s scribbled on a chalkboard. It required motivating, challenging, inspiring, collaborating, and disciplining. It was all about the people, not just basketball plays.

The other side of the job that I hadn't anticipated was the administrative work. The amount of planning and organization needed to keep the team running was astronomical. It felt like being the CEO of a small company and also a single mother of 12 kids. I had to stay on top of all their needs beyond the court, from academics to their health, future plans, breakups, and lack of discipline. I had to change how I did the job—I needed to approach my next coaching season more strategically, with a well-thought-out plan, and not just go in every week and rely on spontaneous decisions. Meticulous preparation and countless hours had to be dedicated behind the scenes during the summer, long before we ever set foot on the court. The unseen labour in the off-season had to be laid as a foundation for success.

What kept me going was that I didn't have another job prospect, as well as my inherent desire to put my master's thesis to the test. It was an opportunity to put into practice the years of study and preparation I had dedicated myself to. So, despite the rough start, I held onto the clear picture in my mind of transforming our team into national champions. At the conclusion of my first season, some players left the team voluntarily, others were informed that we were moving in a different direction, and some mutually agreed not to return, acknowledging that new recruits would likely take their playing time. Ultimately, we found ourselves with only three returning players—a modest foundation to build upon in our second year.

After a challenging first season, I was ready and had the time during the off-season to plan out the vision for the team in detail.

TIME-OUT

Researchers have found that good coaches know the right time to remove athletes who are not buying into their team vision, although determining this timing is one of the least understood aspects of coaching psychology.[1]

CHAPTER 3

Creating a Plan

"Plan for what is difficult while it is easy; do what is great while it is small."
—SUN TZU

O ne of the crucial steps in turning a vision into reality is crafting a well-structured and detailed plan of action. This plan becomes the driving force behind the team or organization; it was a crucial part of how Coach Barnett accomplished what he did with Northwestern. Merely dreaming, hoping, or envisioning the future is insufficient on its own. Many individuals fail to see their dreams come to fruition because they fail to create a tangible and actionable strategy. To this day, I passionately advocate that the success of a vision is directly tied to the hours dedicated to preparing and implementing a written plan of action.

After completing my first season, I crafted a comprehensive five-year plan, outlining the strategic steps my team would take to rise from worst to first. I chose a five-year timeline because all of our new recruits would then be in their final year with our program. To visualize this plan, I envisioned a staircase with five distinct steps, each representing a year of dedicated work. Starting with the ultimate goal in mind—winning a national championship in year five—I worked backwards, setting up significant milestones that built upon the successes of the previous year, until I was brought back to where we were currently standing: last in the league. I then worked at finding motivational themes to label each year's journey, aiming to provide a sense of direction for the players. These themes served as our purpose and mission for every season. Figure 2 is a summary of this plan.

YEAR 1	2005–06: Year of Foundation

Goal: Learn and build the foundation. Set and adhere to new standards: mentally, physically, athletically and academically.
Priority: Recruiting. Most of the finances are targeted in this direction.

- Engineer beginning of transformation culture through renewed work ethic and positive attitudes.
- Change the mentality of the players' standards through new rules, regulations, and demands.
- Improve the profile and reputation of our program by our involvement in the community, our performances, and our dedication to varsity events.

YEAR 2	2006–07: Year of Transformation

Goal: Transform. Make play-offs with a very young team of players newly recruited.
Priority: Recruiting and nurturing of the 9–9 new players we will have.

- Complete the transformation of our appearance, character, and culture.
- **Lead:** returning players have bought in the change established by the program and are living examples of our renewed culture and values.
- **Mold:** new players adopt our standards immediately. It is not a change for them but simply how things are run.

YEAR 3	2007–08: Year of Solidification

Goal: Take form. Make it to the conference final tournament.
Priority: Financial resources will be used towards competing at higher levels, against better teams, in both Canada and the USA.

- **Training:** this team will be the nucleus with which we will win a National Championship.
- **Repetition:** drill systems and standards. It's time ti reinforce all we have learned in terms of lifestyles, training, systems and philosophies.
- **Team spirit and cohesiveness:** our team will acquire a championship mentality.

YEAR 4	2008–09: Year of Realization

Goal: Perform. Win our conference title and make it to the National Championship.
Priority: Most finances will be used towards helping with Athletic Scholarships and supporting players already in the system.

- **Win:** This skill must be learned at the conference level to be repeated at the national level.
- **Experience:** we need to be at nationals, so we learn how to win it.

YEAR 5	2009–10: Year of Celebration

Goal: Celebrate. Win the National Championship.
Priority: Most finances will be used towards helping with Athletic Scholarships and supporting players already in the system.

- **Lifestyle:** athletes are trained to win.
- One focus and uniformed purpose.
- **Recruiting:** most players will be in 4th and 5th year of eligibility.

Figure 2: Five-Year Plan to Win Nationals

Once I had articulated our vision on paper, it allowed all of us to see the bigger picture. However, I knew that simply having this plan written down would not guarantee success. The plan still needed to be executed and bought into. I had to break it down further into actionable steps that could be executed on a monthly, weekly, and daily basis.

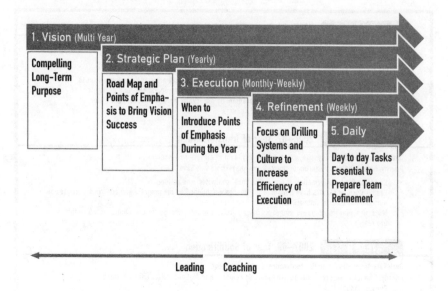

Figure 3: Coach Vallée's Five-Step Coaching Process

Figure 3 illustrates the coaching process (CP) that I employed to develop these actionable steps. It involves a series of indispensable procedures for achieving our goal. Breaking the vision into ever-smaller actions helped us identify specific tasks to be carried out on a yearly basis, then monthly, weekly, and finally daily. Taking the time to develop such a process helped me lead the staff and players in the direction of our ultimate vision. Unlike in my first season, when I flew by the seat of my pants, in my second season, our day-to-day output of energy was spent specifically on reaching the goals I'd prioritized. Developing this method allowed for a clear process to emerge; it became easier for players focus their daily energy, though achieving our desired result was still out of reach.

TIME-OUT

Effectively conveying and executing the coach's vision requires clearly communicating both the vision and the strategic plan to the team members. Research has proven that to sustain such culture, assistant coaches, personnel, and athlete leaders must also uphold the same vision as the leader in their respective roles.[1]

CHAPTER 4

Trusting the Process

"Hold the vision, trust the process."
—UNKNOWN

I n the summer between my first and second seasons, newly armed with both a five-year plan and a strategic plan for the upcoming season, I felt more equipped to change the direction of our program. The first year of the plan was about creating a foundation, which meant working on fundamentals at practice, as well as raising our standards both on and off the court. Now that we had a plan, we had to stick to it—every day, week, and month during the year to come. Trusting that process over the next five years would be critical, especially when the going got tough. "Trust the process" is a key phrase, and I reminded my team of it often, especially when we could barely make a dent in the rankings. It was our motivational anchor as we felt like we were training like champions but still experiencing losing seasons.

Although the mantra "trust the process" was something our team heavily relied upon, it wasn't until much later that the slogan was made popular in the basketball world by fans of the NBA's Philadelphia 76ers. Philadelphians adopted this slogan during a rough patch of franchise history to assure themselves that while things might look bad, they had a plan in place to make it better. This was exactly how I wanted my team to feel. The 76ers GM, Sam Hinkie, implemented a strategic plan in 2013 that focused on long-term success rather than immediate wins. The strategy involved sacrificing short-term victories and talent in exchange for higher draft picks and younger players. The plan eventually produced successful results when the 76ers inked centre and power forward Joel Embiid, the third overall draft pick in 2014, and Ben Simmons, the sought-after first overall pick, in the 2016 NBA draft. Simmons would go on to claim the NBA Rookie of the Year award and became a three-time All-Star, while Embiid became a five-time NBA All-Star and the 2023 league MVP. Hinkie began the process of building up the team around these two core young star players. His vision has had such an impact on the organization that Embiid even nicknamed himself "The Process."

Sam Hinkie's long-term thinking may not have yielded the championship he hoped for; however, the 76ers have made progress and are a strong competitor with momentum in the Eastern Conference.

SELLING THE VISION

As far as our team was concerned, trusting the process was also a slow and difficult learning curve. It was one thing to convince our staff to believe in long-term goals, but to persuade fans, players, and potential recruits was a completely different story. Imagining a championship win, creating a vision, and writing out strategic plans were all crucial steps in the transformation of the University of Windsor women's basketball team. But a major hurdle had yet to be cleared: people had to buy in.

Numerous factors played a role in influencing our group buy-in, but none held more weight than the overwhelming climate of defeated attitudes, negative opinions, and a disbelief that the status quo could be changed. Few alumni showed interest in supporting us financially. Many expressed disappointment in their own experiences and decided they'd rather not get involved. Pessimism was a common theme in their feedback about the program. Fans added to this. During one game, I was taken aback when I saw a sign in the stands mocking our players: "Last Chance U." There were rumours that the motivational phrase "Windsor 2" circulated in our league meaning that other teams had an guaranteed victory (two points in the win column) when playing us. This negativity had taken hold and affected players' attitudes, resulting in low expectations and a defeated mindset. I needed to find a way to change their perspective and rally as many of them as I could behind my vision.

In search of some arguments and ammunition to get my team to buy in, I decided to dig into the program's history. It became clear to me that throughout its existence the University of Windsor women's basketball team had struggled to find success. Prior to 2005, the program had only achieved a winning record in five seasons. However, during my research, I discovered a glimmer of hope: the 1980–81, 1992–93, and 1993–94 seasons had seen notable success. The 1980–81 team even placed third in the western conference. Winning was indeed possible in Windsor. Considering the achievements of women in the 1980s and 1990s, why couldn't we replicate that success in the 2000s? This insight gave me the first piece of persuasive evidence to build support for my vision.

To change the stigma around our potential performance, I decided that additional strategies, such as persuasive presentations, productive

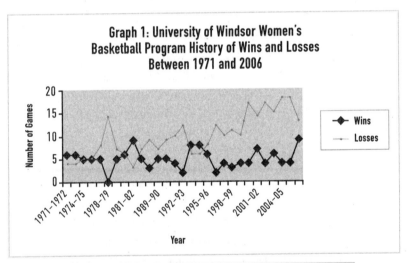

Table 1: Number of Winning Seasons from 1971–2006		
Years	Season	Results (W–L)
1	1971–1972	6–4
2	1972–1973	6–4
3	1980–1981	9–3
4	1992–1993	8–6
5	1993–1994	8–6

Figure 4: History of the University of Windsor Women's Basketball Program

meetings, and celebrating small accomplishments were necessary. So, how did I truly shift the deeply ingrained perception that winning was unattainable in Windsor? This well-known tale sums it up:

Once upon a time, there was a young boy who used to go to the ocean. He noticed an old man at the shore picking up starfish and throwing them into the ocean. He approached the man and called out, "May I ask why you are throwing starfish into the ocean?"

"Because the sun is up, and the tide is going out. If I don't throw them in, they'll die," responded the old man.

Upon hearing this, the young boy exclaimed, "Do you not realize that there are miles and miles of beach and there are starfish along every mile? What you are doing isn't going to make a difference!"

At this, the old man bent down, picked up yet another starfish, and threw it into the ocean. As it sank into the waters, he said, "It made a difference for that one."

That was exactly it. I couldn't change the profile and reputation of our basketball team all at once, but the vision would resonate with players one at a time, and they would buy in, be inspired, and change their minds about the potential of the vision. Slowly, with time, we would start noticing a change in how we spoke about our program, how we carried ourselves, and how we played on the court. We would reshape the program one starfish at a time.

TIME-OUT

Business, management and organisational researchers established that transformational leadership can explain why some leaders are more successful than others at gaining commitment from team members. Transformational leadership focuses on building relationships with followers based on emotional, personal, and inspirational exchanges, with the goal of enhancing their performance. One of the key qualities of a transformational leader is the ability to develop and articulate a vision that promotes group cooperation towards a common goal, while also promoting individualized development by creating a supportive environment tailored to each person's needs.[1]

RECRUIT PLAYERS WHO ALREADY BUY IN

I knew that with a fresh start, getting a collective buy-in would be easier. With only three players returning for my second season, we had the opportunity to purposefully redefine the culture of our team by focusing on new athletes who would buy in. Our five-year vision became the cornerstone of our recruiting efforts. We introduced it to potential recruits, provided them with a copy, and emphasized the silver lining: coming to Windsor meant we were committed to moulding each player into a national champion. Our criteria for selecting recruits went beyond just improving team performance, although that was undoubtedly one of our goals. We specifically sought individuals who would fully accept our vision and align with the culture we aimed to establish. Collaboration, hard work, accountability, dedication, and trust were the values we prioritized during the recruiting process. Let me be clear, talent remained a crucial factor in our decision-making. However, we also passed on exceptionally gifted athletes who did not embody our values. There were two instances where we had to let go of incredibly talented individuals, even a local star, due to incompatible personality traits.

We signed ten new players, most of whom were recruited during the off-season. It was expected that these players wouldn't be the most talented, as our school's ranking made it challenging to attract the most sought-after players. Thankfully, talent and character slowly started to merge as we continued to trust in the process of building our team. I remember signing Raelyn Prince, our first recruit of significance, before my second year. She was a six-foot-two centre who sat in my office, trying to make sense of my sales pitch. "Okay, so you are telling me that the team has not made playoffs, but that if I sign here, we will win a national championship in five years?" I nodded yes, and to my relief, it satisfied her. I knew I was lucky to get her, and I really wanted her to experience the transformation of our program. She ended up being the starting centre for our first national championship.

One year later, we signed our first international player. Iva Peklova was another centre; she had played for the Czech Republic national team. At six foot five, she became our tallest and one of our best players. Iva's statement of commitment was quite ironic: "My parents and I would love for me to move to Canada. We have seen pictures of your country, and we think Banff is beautiful!"They did not know that Banff National Park is in the province of Alberta, a good five-hour flight west from Windsor. Upon hearing this, I laughed and responded that we were a tad far from it, but that I would try to organize a tournament nearby so she could visit. As fate would have it, in her final year, Iva won her second national championship in Calgary, Alberta, and she had the chance to visit beautiful Banff National Park.

The end of Iva's career was spectacular, but the beginning was rocky. Upon her arrival in Canada, her international status and impressive stature caught the attention of the media, which led to interviews. When asked why she chose to attend the University of Windsor, her response was both shocking and amusing. Without a hint of hesitation, she deadpanned, "I came here to help Coach Chantal win a national championship." The media members chuckled, with one even commenting, "Aren't you cute!" It was clear they weren't taking her seriously. Offended, Iva looked at me and said, "Isn't that what you told me I was here for?" She later said that it seemed as if people in Windsor didn't believe winning was possible. Reluctantly, I had to admit the truth: they didn't.

As long as we believed wholeheartedly in our vision, it was irrelevant what outsiders thought. Keeping our goal in sight was the only way we would be able to reach it. And although each recruit chose to sign for different reasons, all were compelled by the vision. We also signed a lot of players who had no other offers and were not the most talented—but they were all great character people. We knew that coachable athletes who have a good work ethic, respect authority, and understand their roles help everyone buy in.

TIME-OUT

Great leaders are always thinking about the future, especially if they are taking over a franchise that has stumbled onto hard times. Researchers considered the legacy of Sir Alex Ferguson, the former esteemed manager of Manchester United. Remarkably, Manchester United had not won a Premier League title in nearly 20 years prior to his arrival. Under his control of the franchise, the team won 13 Premier League titles in his 26 seasons: he transformed the

Manchester United Football Club into a dynasty. Using his platform, Ferguson restructured the team's youth development system, infused the organization with younger players, and transformed the culture from that of a social club to an elite football team.[2]

SHORT-TERM PAIN FOR LONG-TERM GAIN

It is very hard to always keep the long-term plan in mind, especially with the pressure of winning and contract renewals. Many times I had to make a very difficult decision to stay aligned with our longer-term goals, and almost failed to. Athlete misconduct is always difficult to navigate. I will never forget when, in my fourth season at the helm of the Lancers team, Raelyn, our starting centre, got in an altercation with one of our assistant coaches, and he kicked her out of practice. The practice continued as planned, but everyone knew that the punishment for being kicked out of practice for misconduct was a suspension from the next game. I went home with this situation stuck in my mind, especially because I had not witnessed what had happened. The next day's game was a must-win if we were to stay in the playoff race, and the thought of competing without Raelyn affected my sleep. Honestly, I didn't want to suspend her. I cared more about winning and making the playoffs than anything else in that moment. I even rationalized that I could play her in this game and penalize her in the following game since we would be facing a weaker opponent. Deep down, however, I knew that wasn't the right thing to do. The next day, as we were getting ready to load the bus, Raelyn arrived. Before she boarded, I stopped her and said, "Hey, no need to load your bag. We are going to head up without you." Until I gave her that instruction, I wasn't sure I would follow through with my decision. There was a noticeable silence for the whole three-hour bus ride.

During the pre-game meeting, I was anxious but stood my ground, saying, "Obviously we are missing Raelyn, so we must find a way to win this game." After designating a new starting centre who was three inches shorter, I added that I trusted that we could find a way to win. Our alternate seized the opportunity and played incredibly well. What followed was an unbelievable effort from our other starters and bench players—everyone stepped up to fill in the gap. The players respected that I had drawn the line, and it had motivated them to play harder. Despite missing our starting centre, we won. I was relieved that a gutsy call had worked in the short term, and it paid even more dividends in the long term. My team showed more respect towards our coaching staff and had a lot more faith in our leadership.

Opting for long-term development of culture over short-term victories requires strength of character and a lot of discipline. "Culture over results" is the responsibility of team leaders, especially in the thick of hard-to-make decisions. This is precisely how coaches gain respect and buy-in for their direction.

TIME-OUT

Difficult athlete behaviours and the issues they create are an inevitable part of sporting life. If left unaddressed, they can create conflict within the team and have serious implications on team outcomes.[3] A similar phenomenon has been found in business research: one bad apple can affect the cohesive functioning of a group by significantly reducing its cooperation levels, if the behaviour is not addressed by a team leader.[4]

FIND A WAY

While one of the toughest challenges was to convince players that Windsor could be a winning team, I also faced opposition from within our own school. I wasn't sure if our entire athletic program was infected with a defeatist culture, or if my bold claims of winning simply seemed absurd to everyone around me. I remember being left speechless when one of my athletic directors advised me that there was no pressure to my job; I should be patient and hope for a winning season . . . within the next ten years. Obviously, expectations were low—if there were any expectations at all.

Several clear obstacles to buy-in were created by other contextual factors. At Windsor, our gymnasiums and athletic facilities were paid for largely by a mandatory athletic fee that is charged to each student attending our university. In exchange, they have access to all recreational services and athletic facilities, including the weight room and gymnasiums. It may seem preposterous that an elite team has to compete with regular students' access to practice and game times—but it is true. The competition for court time even extended beyond our regular student population and involved various university departments, the community, and even our own varsity teams. Sharing space presents a significant limitation that has caused headaches and frustration every year.

One successful strategy we implemented was using local high school gyms. In certain cases, we had to pay a substantial fee to rent a gymnasium from the school board, leaving us with no choice but to launch fundraising efforts to meet our program's training requirements. It would be one thing to have to fundraise to get rid of one limitation, but the challenge did not end there. Lack of access to the varsity weight room also became problematic. In my first year, few varsity Lancer athletes and coaches were occupying the weight room. As other coaches also worked to change their team's culture and demanded their players pay more attention to physical training, all of us ran into problems with access to the weight room. It became impossible to access squat racks; our team would find themselves sharing only two racks with the men's football and hockey teams. Multiple attempts to bring this issue to our administration bore no fruit. So, we decided to outsource our strength and conditioning to a company off-campus. Of course, this meant that we needed to pay for a trainer and for space. This increased our fundraising needs by several thousand dollars per year—a task we chose to face head-on—because of its importance.

Soon, the limitations grew. We saw our access to athletic therapy compromised. Again, we pivoted and developed a strategy that meant hiring specialists from the community, which included physiotherapists, chiropractors, massage therapists, and osteopaths. Funding for these services came from a combination of fundraising, player contributions, and, at times, parents using their personal health care benefit coverage.

I attempted to convince our administration to increase our budget. In the summer before my second season, I presented my exhaustive five-year plan to the athletic director, with the hope of receiving more support and funding. The 30-page document included our goals, needs, rationale, and a clear financial plan that supported a request for an increased budget. I was confident my athletic director would support my plan because it was so thorough, and it made sense. In fact, I had it reviewed by the dean of the Faculty of Human Kinetics for feedback, and with his support, I was thrilled to print a copy and leave it on my athletic director's desk for review. A week later, the phone rang. Expecting to get an invitation to meet with my athletic director, I was stunned to instead have only a short phone call. While my plan was impressive, there would be no budget change. I was upset.

After that call, I adopted a new mentality. If we would not be funded by our university, we would take the matter into our own hands. I decided we would have to fundraise even more each year to pay for every service we needed. Many coaches overlook the importance of managing their program comprehensively. I call this approach "finding a way." The alternative is to become frustrated and resigned, accepting that success is unattainable due to the lack of support. I did not want to be one of these coaches.

TIME-OUT

Research demonstrates that coaches' job satisfaction is influenced by much more than just wins and losses. Key factors such as relationships with athletic directors, recruiting, publicity, the university environment, and budgeting significantly impact coaches' overall satisfaction and well-being.[5]

Table 1 displays our financial needs, imposed by our lack of resources, from the beginning of my time at Windsor. Our fundraising goal was not insignificant. In order to build a national championship program, we needed to bring in $90,000 every year. It was a lofty goal considering the financial crisis the city was experiencing in the mid-2000s, but I had to find a way to raise these funds if I wanted to build a national champion team.

I firmly believe that every vision can become a reality with a well-written plan subdivided into thorough strategic plans that are well executed. After a deep analysis, obtaining additional financial resources, recruiting, and playing top teams in the country became a top priority from year three forward. The stars aligned when I had the opportunity to meet Dr. Jane

Part of exhibition games and tournaments not funded	$30,000
Part of food on the road for players not funded	$9,000
Extra Athletic Scholarship not funded	$15,000
Part of gear and equipment not funded	$5,000
Part of recruiting not funded	$8,000
Part of assistant coaches' salary not funded	$10,000
Gym rentals not funded	$1,000
Strength and conditioning not funded	$12,000
TOTAL	$90,000

Table 1: Team Fundraising Needs

Brindley, the university president's wife, at a school function during year three. Dr. Brindley had experienced the transformative power of being part of the first women's rugby team in her province and understood the lack of financial resources put into women's sports. She showed keen interest in my vision and offered to organize a fundraising event that brought together influential members of the community. During my keynote speech at that event, I presented our plan, and to my astonishment, the audience responded with a standing ovation. The event generated numerous donations to our program and also gained us a significant increase in fan support at our games. It was a powerful validation of our vision and a remarkable turning point for the program.

As I continued to share our needs and our plan, another breakthrough occurred in year four. Dr. Richard Peddie, a prominent University of Windsor alumnus and at the time the CEO and president of Maple Leaf Sports and Entertainment, came to town to speak to our men's football and basketball teams exclusively. Although I wasn't invited to meet him, bravely I positioned myself near the exit door of the event to seize the opportunity to introduce myself. As he was leaving, I caught his attention by waving and shaking his hand. To my surprise, he stopped and said, "Really nice to meet you, Chantal. I've heard a lot of great things about you and your work with the team." He added his willingness to help if I ever needed anything. It was a brief conversation, but I managed to mention that our biggest challenge was finding financial resources before he was moved along by my athletic director to continue with his meetings.

Less than a week later, I received a letter from Dr. Peddie at my office, along with a cheque for $3,000, wishing me good luck for the season. As we kept winning, new letters and cheques would appear. This marked the beginning of a relationship that would evolve into a lasting friendship over the years. Remarkably, Richard later went on to purchase all of our championship rings, even jokingly remarking, "The Raptors and the Maple Leafs never got me a ring, but Chantal did." (The Raptors did win the NBA championship later, in 2019.)

COMMITMENT

We now had a way to generate money through several annual fundraisers; we also had recruits. Though they may not have been the most talented prospects out there, they had agreed to come to Windsor and buy into our process. At that point, all we needed was a star to help get us over the hump. I worked diligently at recruiting the best talent coming out of Canada and even the United States. It was an uphill battle; it felt like every single player I talked to ended up passing us over. I was lucky in my second year at Windsor: destiny aligned the stars once more to reward my recruiting efforts.

Dranadia Roc, a player I knew from my coaching days at Vanier College in Quebec, was seeking a transfer back from Florida State University (FSU). Dranadia was a standout player, even making Canada's senior women's national team at the young age of 17. After one year in the NCAA, she reached out to me, expressing her desire to find a supportive and secure environment to continue her basketball journey. I knew that if anyone could champion my vision and make a significant impact at Windsor, it was Dranadia. I welcomed her with open arms.

Dranadia epitomized trust in the process and unwavering commitment to our vision. On paper, our second season may have been deemed a failure, but we were laying the foundation for something greater, and Dranadia played a pivotal role in that. She embraced our mission and set the example for the team. Dranadia shattered numerous Lancer records, earning the title of Ontario University Athletics Rookie of the Year in her first season back and later becoming a league all-star. She led us as our captain when we clinched our first provincial championship and competed in our inaugural national championship appearance. While she never won a national championship title during her time with us, the program's success would not have been possible without her contributions. She went on to play professionally in Iceland for a year and worked for the Toronto Raptors before joining the Toronto Police Service as a constable. To this day, she still plays basketball with the police force.

One story that exemplifies Dranadia's commitment to my coaching philosophy took place on a breezy Saturday afternoon in the fall of my third season. Dranadia, now our all-Canadian player, was late for the bus for our second of back-to-back games in Ottawa. I was feeling really tense because I did not want to leave the hotel without her. She was our best player, and it was not uncommon for her to score 30 points in a game. As everyone became more anxious, I finally told the bus driver to leave. Even though I had a knot in my stomach, I knew I had to be firm. At some point during warm-up, Dranadia joined the team on the court. I do not know how she got to the game, and I did not play her in the first half. At halftime, we were trailing by double digits. In the locker room, I ended our halftime meeting by looking at her and telling her she was starting the second half. She did not come off the floor for the entire second half, and she scored above her average points, leading us to a comeback victory. Thankfully, we won, which helped justify the decision I had made to leave her behind. However, it was an excruciating mental battle for me throughout the warm-up and first half. Leaving her behind was a tough decision for me, and a tough lesson for her, but I can attest to the fact that no one in this group was ever late again. It was clear that the message had been sent and the standard had been set in terms of behavioural expectations. That moment represented another example of making tough decisions based on my long-term vision as opposed to seeking a short-term win.

If you think that I simply got lucky with meeting the right people, receiving timely donations, and landing top-notch recruits, you're probably right. I can't deny it. And it was all pivotal to the program's transformation. The point, however, is these fortuitous events would not have happened without a clear plan and a clear vision. Throughout our journey towards realizing our vision, a vital aspect of growth for my team was grasping the significant power of our intention when setting goals. I made it a point to annually educate my team on the different levels of intentions required to succeed in pursuing a dream or vision. The diagram below served as a valuable tool in teaching the psychological focus and unwavering determination necessary to achieve a goal. Intentions possess varying degrees of power, influence, and effectiveness; it is essential for us to be mindful of our intention levels when embarking on a project or wholeheartedly embracing a vision.

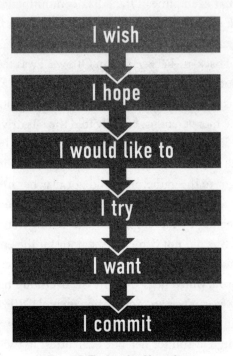

Figure 5: The Levels of Intention

The commitment human beings have for a dream or vision can be understood through six key phrases, each representing a different level of intention, from a weaker resolution or desire (*I wish*) to the strongest (*I commit*). The highest level of determination or desire is commitment, which is characterized by active engagement and by no option to turn back. It is the most powerful form of intention a person can embody in their thoughts and in the physical world. While many would like to or even want to win, only a select few are willing to devote the energy and unwavering effort required over an extended period of time. Commitment is having a player at FSU who remembers playing for you and knows that a clear direction and high-level culture are part of who you are as a coach, so she calls you back. Commitment is taking a deep breath and finding the courage to show up uninvited to Richard Peddie's talk and introduce yourself.

Commitment made my mentality to "find a way" possible. Dranadia was a tangible living example of commitment as well. Despite facing significant losses, she diligently worked long hours as the team's captain to study scouting reports on our opponents, meet with her teammates, improve her skills, and forge relationships with the community in Windsor. She also took on the responsibility of scoring enough points to help us win, one game at a time.

Before long, our players embraced the same level of commitment. They willingly woke up at 5:30 a.m. to hit the court and then proceeded to the weight room from 6:30 to 7:30 a.m. By the time 8:30 a.m. rolled around, they had completed two training sessions, enjoyed breakfast, freshened up, and were seated in their first class of the day. They adhered to a strict schedule that sometimes included additional meetings for game analysis or community service outings, all before our regular team practices in the evening.

Once the competitive season commenced, there were times we returned home from away games as late as 2 or 3 a.m. Yet the following morning, our players dutifully attended their classes and then showed up for evening practice. During the summers, they remained in Windsor, dedicating themselves to daily training and participating in two summer leagues. This unwavering commitment persisted throughout their entire university careers, ultimately leading to a remarkable transformation.

One of my favourite illustrations of commitment is the Vikings' embodiment of the principle. The Vikings were known to be ruthless warriors who terrorized Europe from the late 700s to the 1100s. After landing on any inhabited island that they were aiming to conquer, they would burn the boats they sailed in on. With the image of their own boats in flames at their backs, they would advance towards the battle, into the unknown, carrying a powerful message: "We win, or we perish!" The action of burning their boats reinforced and dictated an extreme sense of commitment. There was no turning back. You can also bet that a sense of fear infiltrated their opponents at the sight of the burning boats. This was the level of commitment necessary to move a basketball program through a transformative process.

THE TURNING POINT

During year three, we set a specific goal that would mark a turning point in the history of the program: reaching ten wins in a single season, a record yet to be achieved. The target resonated with our players, and they united in support for this shared objective. This short-term goal became the driving force behind our team's motivation; we were determined to etch our names into the annals of Lancer history. Despite the fact that winning ten games would still result in a losing season, we recognized the power of setting a small, attainable goal that emphasized positivity and incremental progress. We dedicated significant time to discussing and promoting this milestone. It served as the cornerstone of our strategy, nurturing our motivation even during challenging moments. We constantly reminded ourselves that surpassing this record would immortalize our current team, ensuring our place in the history books. This was the turning point for our collective journey. And true to our aspirations, we exceeded our initial goal, triumphantly clinching a total of 14 wins that season—a remarkable feat that marked our inaugural winning season.

We learned a valuable lesson during our journey: sometimes things can worsen before they improve. In our initial year, we managed to secure nine victories, but that number dwindled to just six in our second year. If we had given up following that setback, I might not have continued as the coach, and this book would not exist. The profound wisdom gained from this experience is that encountering difficulties is not an indication of a flawed vision. On the journey towards realizing a vision, it is all too common for individuals to give up just before reaching that pivotal turning point, that beacon of hope, the light at the end of the tunnel. Setbacks and challenges can breed discouragement, leading people to doubt the feasibility of their goals. Reflecting on the past, I am immensely grateful that despite the obstacles we encountered, I remained steadfast in my commitment to Windsor, channelling my Viking spirit. And I was not alone in this pursuit. We all set ablaze the boats that tied us to the possibility of giving up. As you can imagine, when the fruits of our labour finally started to materialize, and we started to win, it ignited an even fiercer determination within us.

QUARTER BREAK

Four Keys to Building a Successful Vision

1. **DARE.** Start with the end in mind. Think about a desired outcome or a long-term dream that could be accomplished. It doesn't have to be realistic by so-called real world standards. Write down this dream or goal, and summarize it in one sentence. Read it out loud. Could you even draw it? Images are a great way to solidify what you see in your mind's eye. This will become your vision.

2. **SLOW DOWN YOUR MIND.** Sitting down and thinking may seem counterproductive, but activities such as reading, journaling, drawing, and praying or meditating are essential steps towards success. During these activities, you will be inspired and guided towards what steps to take next. This step is essential to using imagery effectively.

3. **PLAN.** Create a definite plan to carry out your vision. To do so, set intermediate yearly goals, like steps that move backwards from the end goal to your starting point. These intermediate goals should be realistic and achievable and lead directly to realizing your long-term vision. These intermediate steps become your mission.

4. **COMMIT.** People follow a vision when their leader combines words with actions. Commitment involves trusting the process. Persist, and adjust if needed. Your journey will likely get worse before it gets better. Be committed. Don't quit; find a way. Stay the course. Burn your boat.

COACH INSIGHT: It is never too late to start over or to pursue your dreams. Our own limiting beliefs are what impede change, transformation, and achievements. One of my colleagues earned her PhD and completed an Ironman in her sixties.

LOOK AHEAD TO THE SECOND QUARTER

Leaders often struggle to realize that they may be the ones standing in the way of their own success—and that of their team. Keep reading to discover how I faced this challenge and to learn practical ways to break through these barriers.

SECOND QUARTER
THE COACH

"Our greatest glory is not in never falling, but in rising every time we fall."
—OLIVER GOLDSMITH

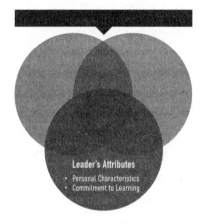

Leader's Attributes
- Personal Characteristics
- Commitment to Learning

The journey to becoming a successful leader requires a deep level of introspection and a willingness to seek out criticism and mentorship from others. It is not about what a leader does but who they are at their core. Sure, these remarkable leaders possess both the technical expertise and tactical knowledge of their craft, but they also possess exceptional soft skills. They excel in people, social, and communication skills and hold a high degree of emotional intelligence. They strive for excellence and are always hungry for knowledge, self-improvement, and growth.

Our research model places this within the leader's attributes category, highlighting that expert and successful leaders exhibit a wide range of personal characteristics along with an insatiable drive for continuous learning.

CHAPTER 5

The Limiting Factor

"There's no more powerful lesson than knowing that your setbacks will one day help you succeed."

—RESHMA SAUJANI

ON THE WAY UP

A true story about two brothers has impacted me ever since I read about them while researching for my master's degree. Many years ago, there was young schoolboy named Walter who had a passion for doodling, daydreaming, and drawing. He spent hours sketching and creating new characters in his own imaginary worlds. His older brother Roy was more pragmatic and very good at mathematics. As time went on, Roy became a successful banker while his younger brother kept drawing. One day, Walter, never shy of thinking big, contacted Roy to ask him to make an investment that would help make one of his dreams come true. He believed that his characters could come to life and inspire people of all ages. With a vision and a plan, both brothers developed Walt Disney Productions and later the massive success of Walt Disney World.

Success stories like Walt Disney's often tend to gloss over the setbacks and difficulties that were faced along the way. This can create a false impression that success is achieved in a straightforward and easy fashion. While the positive outcomes of Disney's accomplishments are most often talked about, a more in-depth analysis of his story is more revealing. Walt Disney's first major venture, Laugh-O-Gram Studio, opened in 1921 in Kansas City, Missouri, and produced fairy-tale shorts, cartoons, and a short film—and it seemed that success was on the horizon. Instead, the company was bankrupt by 1923 after being cheated by New York–based distributors. Walter then made the move to California, teamed up with his brother Roy, and founded Disney Brothers Studio (soon renamed Walt Disney Studios). They were off to the races with a new investor and started producing animated films featuring Oswald the Lucky Rabbit. After a dispute, however, in 1928, their financier pulled, taking the rights to all their cartoons and several employees with them. The brothers were forced to pivot—and it was out of this creative pressure that the iconic Mickey Mouse was born. By 1940, Walt Disney Studios was booming, and the company moved into a large production studio in Burbank, California. One year later, there was an animator strike, with many resigning or being fired. It took the company over a year to get back on track. When the Disneyland theme park opened its doors in Anaheim in 1955, it was a smashing success—but its opening days were marred by counterfeit tickets, massive overcrowding, traffic jams, and food and beverage shortages. In 1971, the Walt Disney Company expanded into Florida with the opening of Magic Kingdom Park as the first in a series of Orlando theme parks. And in the saddest setback of all, Walter died in 1966 from lung cancer, while the park was still under construction. He never got the chance to see his biggest dream come true. It was Roy who saw his brother's vision to fruition.

Magic Kingdom, with its cartoon characters brought to life, saw daylight following the pursuit and realization of a 51-year dream. Despite facing setbacks and challenges along the way, Walter never lost sight of his vision and worked to create beloved characters that have become an integral part of popular culture and continue to inspire generations of artists, dreamers, and innovators.

When I interviewed the top coaches as part of my master's degree, I was left with an underlying impression that these leaders formed a plan, executed it, and reached victory in quite a linear manner. I was unaware that managing people and a business could be so terribly messy until I started my work as a university coach. When it didn't go smoothly, my naïveté created self-doubt in my capacity to lead and be successful like the leaders I revered. With limited experience in management, I often found myself facing challenges that left me feeling overwhelmed and disheartened. It seemed like every turn brought a new issue to contend with. Just when I thought I had things under control, another problem would surface. The pace of daily decision-making, both on and off the court, was challenging to say the least.

FIRST NATIONAL CHAMPIONSHIP APPEARANCE

Just like the journeys of Walt Disney and all the successful coaches I had interviewed, my journey to success was anything but a smooth, straight line. In my fourth season with the Lancers, I thought we had turned a corner as a program and that the struggles of building a winning culture were behind us. We qualified for our first-ever national championship in year four of my coaching career at Windsor. It was being held in Regina, Saskatchewan. When playoffs began, a camera crew was following our journey in hopes of turning our imminent underdog story into a film, and I was quite anxious about making it happen. After a brilliant Elite Eight performance on Friday, we lost to the host team in the Final Four on Saturday. As Canadian national championship brackets go, we were then slated to play for a bronze medal the next day.

On that Sunday afternoon, we were determined not to leave empty-handed despite being deflated by the previous day's loss. We played with heart, passion, and led the entire game. However, in the fourth quarter, the momentum shifted, and doubt began to creep in. As the clock wound down, a powerful fear of losing overtook me. I froze. The uproar from the bench snapped me back to reality. Many voices were shouting, trying to pass on the message that something needed to be done: *now*. Where had I gone for the last few seconds? I tried to tune in to what my assistants were saying, but I could not hear clearly. I made a hasty decision to ask my point guard to foul the opposing team. This proved to be one of the worst coaching decisions of my career. We lost the game in complete chaos. The players, assistant coaches, and fans all knew that we could have won with better end-of-game management. It was a devastating loss.

A heavy silence surrounded our team as we lined up to shake hands and congratulate the new bronze medallists. I felt so horrible and embarrassed that I could not look anyone in the eye. I could feel my team's disapproval. My inability to lead under pressure had just ripped the medal out of my players' hands. Dissatisfaction with my leadership and coaching grew among our players.

TIME-OUT

Research in sport psychology has continuously demonstrated that athlete performance and satisfaction are influenced by their coaches' knowledge, skills, and behaviours. A 2017 study discovered that all the coaches were unsatisfied with their first experience coaching at a national championship. Most of them felt they did not have the knowledge to prepare the athletes and support staff for these high-level competitions. Interestingly, none of the participants won the national title the first time they participated at the tournament, and they all felt personally responsible for their team underperforming at that championship. They reflected on their experiences and identified aspects that needed to be improved.[1]

The frantic loss at our first national championship appearance was a crushing blow, but the aftermath was worse. The team had been on the cusp of greatness, and with everyone returning the following season, we were poised to make history and win next year's national championship. Then in what seemed like the blink of an eye, everything fell apart. Two of our star players, the backbone of the team, unexpectedly left. I could feel the tension between us as I attempted in vain to convince them otherwise. The team was left reeling, with a massive hole in the lineup that seemed impossible to fill. Our program would be relegated to the middle of the pack, at best. We would have to start over again. It was a bitter pill to swallow.

I could not help but feel an immense sense of failure as I faced the harsh reality that my plan to win a national championship within five years had fallen apart. The grand vision that once looked so promising on paper now seemed like nothing more than a pipe dream. As the leader of the team, I had to acknowledge that I lacked the necessary skills to manage people effectively and provide clear direction in times of crisis. As my program had grown to compete at the level of the country's best teams, I had become the limiting factor to my team's success.

That summer was a struggle for me. Overwhelmed and on edge, I felt as if I had hit a wall. The weight of the team's fate loomed over me. I knew something had to change, but I didn't know where to start. I suffered in silence until I couldn't take it anymore. In a moment of desperation, I turned to prayer and let it all out. The release lifted the darkness, and my mind began to clear. Most importantly, it created space for me to receive advice. I dove into books and articles, seeking guidance on how to overcome struggles as a leader. That's when I stumbled upon imposter syndrome, a theory that explained how I had been feeling.

THE IMPOSTER

Pauline Rose Clance and Suzanne Imes first identified imposter syndrome or imposter phenomenon in the late 1970s as a psychological experience that affects high achievers or perfectionists who feel inadequate despite evidence that they are skilled and capable. This insidious pattern is often observed in highly motivated individuals who aim for excellence while harbouring a deep-seated fear of being exposed as frauds. Although I had not heard of this theory when I took over the team, I can attest that in moments of difficulty, obstacle, or failure, I felt like an imposter trying to navigate my way through the situation as best I could.

TIME-OUT

As the name *imposter syndrome* suggests, a person with it questions their own competencies and feels like a failure even if they meet 99 percent of their goal, states Dr. Valerie Young, an expert on the topic. Research demonstrates that imposter syndrome is present in individuals in different fields, such as medicine, and affects women more often than men. In particular, women of colour at elite universities are often afflicted with impostor syndrome.[2]

Realizing that very competent individuals in all spheres of life were having similar experiences took a load of pressure and guilt off my shoulders. Sure,

I had been the limiting factor in our first national championship appearance, but this new knowledge made me open up to the fact that maybe I was competent after all, just inexperienced. It allowed me to relax and be less hard on myself. First, I had to acknowledge my weaknesses and work on my end of game management. Second, maybe I wasn't an imposter, just embarrassed about my mistakes. It made me wonder if other coaches had experienced similar feelings. I went back to the research I had done at McGill University, and I read something that had not resonated for me before. It had been there all along: the coaches I had interviewed had talked about mistakes they had made, players being mad at them, and the need to re-evaluate their leadership as they built their team.

One of the four categories of my research findings was leader's attributes, which detailed their personal characteristics and commitment to learning. The missing piece of my puzzle became apparent to me: in my hastiness to get the team to the top, I had completely lost the point of the coach's journey. Self-reflecting, adjusting, growing, acknowledging mistakes, and striving to get better were all part of the process, as well recognizing the gaps in my performance and taking steps to bridge them. These words from one successful coach I'd interviewed summed it all up:

> I made mistakes with players like everyone else, and I would like to take back some words that I have said or some actions ... But it is a part of life to accept that we are in roles where, in some respect, we learn through trial and error. We do not always know what the right solution is, so we have to take risks.

Expert coaches *did* openly talk about making mistakes, including those of leadership and management, and about learning from their early coaching experiences. They valued self-evaluation during and after games, practices, and seasons and saw it as part of the learning process. The more I reread the transcripts of the coaches I had interviewed, the more their words proved they were constantly at work on themselves. How did they improve their leadership traits, communication styles, decision-making skills, and more? They worked to become open-minded, balanced, composed, caring, and genuinely interested in their athletes.

The leader's attributes category now had a completely different meaning than when I had first written about it five years earlier. I had put so much emphasis on the three other categories of the research findings (vision, organizational skills, players' individual growth) that I hadn't considered my own development as a leader. I had put in place what I thought was a culture of growth in my players by considering their individuality and the importance to treat them holistically. But I had not spent much time looking inward, nor had I mastered how to work on myself. This, combined with my inexperience in management, opened room for many ego-driven decisions, which were detrimental to the health of our team and culture. I simply wasn't aware of it—yet.

The summer between my fourth and fifth seasons marked a turning point. Despite our hard work over the last four years, we lost a medal at nationals and two of our star players during the off-season. It left our program on the brink of collapse. This forced me to confront myself as a coach and as a person. I knew that in order to transform my team and take them to the next level, I had to first transform myself.

I decided to look for help.

PREPARE FOR THE STORM

It wasn't long before my desire to learn brought new people into my life in a process that felt almost magical. Pastor Mary Templer changed my perspective during an afternoon coffee chat. "As a leader," she said, "your job is and will always be to navigate and manage one crisis after another. It is not a matter of if drama will happen, but when." It was like a light bulb went off when I heard this. "Expect drama" became my new understanding of a deeper layer of leadership and guiding people through challenges. As a coach, I couldn't control everything, but I could control how I responded. Strong leaders are the ones who can manage one crisis after another without becoming emotionally drained. They expect crisis and use it as an opportunity to improve themselves and their team.

That discussion normalized the challenges I was facing. Players becoming ill or injured, not showing up to practice, quitting, feeling disgruntled, becoming academically ineligible, moving on to the workforce, dealing with homesickness . . . these things did not define who I was as a leader. Rather, they were situations that created opportunities to brilliantly manage our team and ourselves. Being prepared to face crisis meant that these crises would no longer sneak up and beat the shit out of me. Chaos and drama? They're simply part of the job. Realizing this helped me face difficult, uncontrollable situations with a better emotional outlook: it became "Drama happens," instead of "What did I do wrong?"

A few weeks later, a good friend came to visit Windsor. Claire Moon was a former NCAA Division 1 coach that I had met when our teams had played exhibition games against each other. What I appreciated most about her was her ability to tell someone the truth without sugar-coating it. Claire's words challenged me to manage pressure-filled moments during games. She told me to imagine being the captain of a ship that was headed towards a storm. Two things could happen: the ship would sink, or it would stay afloat. But while in the storm, should the captain react by *describing* the storm? "The waves are ten feet tall; water is on the deck; we are slowly sinking; we're all going to drown!" Obviously not. We would expect the captain to control their emotions and give very clear and precise directions as to how to manoeuvre *through* the storm. "Reef the sails, bend the storm sails, tow warps." In her signature direct manner, Claire asked, "What kind of captain are you?" I was guilty of being overwhelmed in a storm, rather than guiding my crew. Claire's visit urged me to move out of my current storm. Her metaphor remains in my head to this day, continually helping me to steady my ship. In a storm, clear directions change momentum and turn setbacks into comebacks. This was right on point with regards to my end-of-game management. I had to increase my knowledge on what to say and how to adjust in crisis situations.

As summer moved along, the universe continued to send me teachers—even as I vacationed in Thailand. As soon as I landed, I was struck by the devastation caused by the tsunami that had hit the coast of the Indian Ocean five years prior. The bustling marketplace areas were adorned with pictures of the aftermath, serving as a reminder of the immense damage and loss of life. Despite the fact that nature had seemingly restored itself, there was a palpable solemnity that hung over Phuket's city centre. In an effort to understand the extent of the damage, I decided to take a ferry to the picturesque Phi Phi Islands. There, I discovered that on the morning of December 26, 2004, a three-metre-high wave had wreaked havoc on much of the inhabited part of the island, killing a majority of the local community.

It was during this stay that I met a young man named Boa, whose story is captivating. Boa experienced unimaginable loss during the tragedy but found a way to heal and move forward. As we kept talking, I wanted to understand how he dealt with grief, guilt, and regret. Surely my issues surrounding basketball paled in comparison with his life experience, but almost as if he had read my mind, he offered, "I healed through a breathing technique that makes me let go and focus on the present moment." His words struck a chord. I had first heard of the idea of "the present moment" while reading *Sacred Hoops: Spiritual Lessons of a Hardwood Warrior* by Phil Jackson. Jackson, one of my all-time favourite coaches, is the former triumphant coach of both the Chicago Bulls and Los Angeles Lakers. He used Zen Buddhist, Christian, and Indigenous spiritual practices in his coaching. Jackson revealed how he taught his players to develop a clear mind in games by practising being present, which meant not overthinking, and staying calm in the midst of chaos. It meant not worrying about the future or remaining stuck in the past. How exactly he had achieved this, I had never quite understood.

Boa continued, "During a long inhalation, you allow your emotions to come up and be experienced fully. This may include sadness, worry, regrets—any stress that remains in your body or anything that doesn't sit well with you from the past. When exhaling, let the emotion go out with the air." He was showing me by pointing at his solar plexus. "You have to let the emotions trapped there come out with your breath," he added. The practice of not suppressing an emotion or a thought but rather feeling it, then visualizing letting it go was something I had never heard of before. I had so many difficult emotions and fear trapped inside that I continued to practise this technique as I left the Phi Phi Islands, in hopes of finding relief. As the days went by, my situation slowly improved; I carried with me a newfound appreciation for the power of breath, letting go, and living in the present moment. I have even taught this technique to my team, and we subsequently have used it in time-outs, when pressure and fear are at high levels. Later in life, I adopted a daily practice of breathing and mediation that is focused on strengthening my nervous system.

Back in the summer between my fourth and fifth season, in the pursuit of excellence, I had gotten lost in the external world, constantly worrying about situations I could not control. I would say this held true for a long time in my coaching career. However, practising the art of letting go through breathing finally convinced me that true solutions come from within. Never giving up on oneself while letting go of disappointments was the best way to move forward successfully.

There is a saying: "When the student is ready, the teacher appears." By the end of the long six months of our off-season, I had met many teachers, and I felt invigorated about starting my fifth season as the head coach. The teachers who had been sent my way throughout the summer had such significant influence on me that I decided to take it a step further and find a professional mentor. I also decided to seek counselling on how to deal with grief and stress, as well as how to improve my overall leadership and communication. I wanted to grow so I would never again be the limiting factor to my team's success. This acknowledgement brought me peace and enough resolve to continue my journey.

TIME-OUT

Breathing-based therapies have roots stretching back hundreds of years. In the face of the demanding pace of modern existence, these practices help us to let go of the past, cultivate mindfulness, and reduce stress. Among the multitude of suggestions from experts, one simple piece of advice persists: learn the art of breathing.[3]

CHAPTER 6

An Empire of Mentors

"Train yourself to let go of everything you are afraid to lose."

—YODA

FIND YOUR YODA

As a passionate fan of science fiction, I have always been mesmerized by the captivating stories that take place in vast and extraordinary universes. *Star Wars* captured my imagination from a young age; George Lucas created epic tales of courage, hope, and the fight between good and evil. But it wasn't just the fantastical settings or the thrilling action scenes that drew me in; it was the wisdom and insight that his characters imparted, especially the wise and powerful Jedi master Yoda.

Yoda's teachings on the Force and the importance of selflessness are a powerful message in a world that prioritizes success and personal achievement. Yoda's lesson is clear: true greatness lies in serving others and seeking personal growth for the greater good. Through Luke Skywalker's journey, we see the transformation that occurs when the mentee's focus shifts from personal ambition to a higher calling, a path of service and sacrifice that brings about profound growth and transformation.

I wanted to find my Yoda.

I contacted our national organization, Canada Basketball, and asked if they could suggest someone who might be willing to take me on as a mentee. I wanted someone with a lot of life experience who had learned to navigate difficult roads successfully. I requested a specific coach, but they provided me with someone very different. In fact, I admit that I would not have picked him out of a list of names if they had given me the choice. That someone, however, became pivotal in our team's success story.

TIME-OUT

Mentoring is a concept that dates back to ancient times, tracing as far back as Greek mythology over 2,700 years ago. Odysseus entrusted his son Telemachus to the goddess Athena, who disguised herself in human form as an old friend of Odysseus. Athena acted as a counsellor and helper, guiding Telemachus towards his goals. Today, research has shown that having a mentor can greatly benefit individuals in any field[1] and that successful people have had one or more mentor-like figures who have influenced their lives in significant ways.[2] The key aspects of mentoring have been defined in nine verbs: model, empathize, nurture, teach, organize, respond, inspire, network, and goal-set.[3]

DON McCRAE

Don McCrae, a retired coach with an impressive track record, had achieved success at the men's university level, winning a national championship, and as a women's coach, setting the all-time best Canadian senior women's national team finish with a fourth in a world championship. When I was introduced to Don, I couldn't help but feel apprehensive. He was 71 years old and lived several hours away from Windsor; I wondered if partnering with him was the right decision. However, I had no other options, so I accepted his help. Little did I know, it would turn out to be one of the best decisions of my life. I vividly remember knocking on Don's door for the first time. As we sat at his dining table, scribbling diagrams and discussing coaching strategies, I could sense the beginning of a remarkable relationship.

Thanks to Don's guidance, I gained a deeper understanding of the game, team management, and in-game decision-making. I have allowed him to criticize me bluntly, always insisting on honest feedback, no matter how harsh. My goal was to become a great leader, and I gave Don the green light to push me as much as needed. I absorbed everything he said and worked tirelessly to improve myself. Don has been a constant resource to me over the years, helping me navigate leadership challenges, coaching decisions, and setbacks. He is committed to maintaining a strong mentoring relationship with me, and he's often driven the seven hours that separate us just to watch our practices and have coffee. Our mentor-mentee relationship has grown so much over the years that I would have never published this book without his thorough review and criticism.

In the second season of our mentoring relationship, Don became more present at practices and games. The team had become quite accustomed to seeing him around. The team was stronger, but I could not quite figure out how to coach a post play that would take advantage of our opponent's strategy. As fate would have it, just before the playoffs, Don paid a visit. In our way stood the University of Ottawa, a well-coached and gritty team that had dominant post players. I decided to give the floor to Don who, back in 1976, had been one of the most powerful post players of our men's senior Olympic team. His teachings were on point, and his drills were perfect.

I was so relieved that my players' trust in me grew through this process. Instead of viewing my decision to pass them on to Don as a weakness, they saw it as a strength. They saw my willingness to put aside my ego and open myself up to the possibility of learning a new way. As a result, we beat Ottawa in the playoffs and were on the path to the national tournament again. From then on, a special relationship developed between my players and my mentor. To this day, everyone is excited when he comes to practice. Don is as much a five-time national champion with the Windsor women's team as any of us.

TIME-OUT

The ability of the mentee to be open—to explore who they are as a leader and discuss their shortcomings and weaknesses—is a sign of trusting and therefore of a healthy mentoring relationship. Research makes it clear that mentees must feel confident that their vulnerability will be met with discretion and the mentor's genuine best intentions.

TOM FOSTER

Don McCrae didn't only affect the way I interacted with my players; he also had a profound influence on my coaching relationships, including how I relate to my long-time assistant coach Tom Foster. To add to Tom's wisdom and experience, Don coached him on how to interact with me in a way that fostered our coaching unity without being overbearing or taking control of the team. For example, by first checking with me prior to giving feedback in practices, it allowed all of us to ensure we relay the same information to players and streamline our demands. Tom has succeeded at never imposing a final decision in any of our team's multiple conundrums, always finishing our brainstorming sessions with his witty quip—"I'm glad *you* have that degree!"—and then walking away. This has never failed to put a smile on my face and always gives me the confidence to tackle whatever challenge lies in my way. Working with Tom has been beneficial for me in more ways than one: increasing my confidence as a human being and teaching me how to be a better assistant coach with our Canadian national team.

I love recounting the story of how we started working together. I wasn't sure how much I should trust him since he was older and more experienced than me in both coaching and life. I thought hiring him might be a precarious choice that could lead to power struggles as to who leads the team. He had been an assistant coach on the men's team for years, and a head coaching change on the men's side had Tom knocking on my door a few minutes before my first-ever official day with the team. I still needed to add to our coaching staff, and since Tom had just introduced himself, I asked, "How would a man with your experience be able to take direction from a younger woman like me?" His response was both funny and reassuring: "I grew up with six sisters, and I was the only boy. I have taken direction from women all my life and can assure you that I take direction well from any woman now." I chuckled. That day Tom walked with me straight to the gym, where I introduced him as the new assistant coach. We sure had our moments as we learned to work together well, but over the years, he has evolved into an incredible mentor, as well as a loyal coach and friend.

Mentoring is an ongoing process and can develop with anyone who fills the role of a trusted advisor, assistant, or friend. In Tom's case, so many years on the road, sharing life stories and ups and downs together, has elevated him to a confidant in my personal life. Perhaps freezing our butts off in Montreal while pushing a bus stuck in 20 inches of snow together has something to do with it—or realizing that I mistakenly rented a yellow school bus for a six-hour trip. (I had two pints of beer delivered to Tom's hotel room as an apology.) I have experienced the trust and mutual respect that comes with a great mentoring relationship, which truly makes or breaks the coaching experience. So, to all those seeking mentorship, keep your eyes open for someone like Tom or Don. They just might change your life.

COUNSEL OF ADVISORS

The addition of mentors has brought nothing but positive changes to my coaching. So much so that I continued to surround myself with a greater number of counsellors. By my sixth season, I had built a counsel of four advisors who helped me with the team on top of my assistant coaches. These advisors were not part of our coaching staff on the floor, but experts in their own areas.

To understand the impact of my counsellors, we're going to jump ahead in our story to the eve of winning our record-breaking fifth consecutive national championship in 2015. It was about −20 degrees Celsius in Quebec City, and the atmosphere at the Lancers headquarters—the room where we met to discuss our game plan—may have been even colder. That night, my analytics coach, Lucas Reindler, and all my other assistants did not see eye to eye. The tension was palpable. My assistants were highly experienced coaches and wanted to keep our usual game plan moving to the finals. Lucas, who had never played on a team and was an engineer by trade, was working hard to show us numbers that proved that if we used our regular hi-lo offence we could not *statistically* win against McGill University. The debate was on, and so was the pressure of winning. It was way past midnight, and the championship final was set for 4 p.m. the next day. With less than 16 hours before game time, you can imagine the look on the coaches' faces when we heard that we could not win unless we changed our offensive approach. My assistants eventually went to bed irritated. I was wired. I could not sleep, so instead I watched game tape most of the night trying to understand my analytics expert's viewpoint. At about 3 a.m., halfway into the third game I'd watched, my eyes opened: I saw what he saw.

By the next morning, I had made up my mind. I went to practice with a game plan that would adjust our offence and put the ball in our guard Korissa Williams's hands more often than our post players'—contrary to our team habits. This was quite an adjustment, but I found a way to slip it in without the players noticing the worried looks on the faces of my assistants. The coaching staff had no other choice but to follow my lead, but they were really upset and I could tell. Yet they knew to rally even when they strongly disagreed. Whenever a decision was made, we stood united.

The waiting time between the shoot-around of the morning and the actual start of the game was excruciating. My assistants were silent on the way back after practice. I knew they felt I was wrong, but no one said much until the game. I was a bit nervous about the decision, but I had learned over the years to encourage a feeling of readiness in my players and staff, so despite how I felt, I projected confidence. That afternoon, on another typically cold Quebec City day, the game was a back-and-forth affair in the first half. McGill, however, could not have prepared for us to not use our post players in our usual manner and instead move the ball to the outside. By the second half, Korissa completely took over. She was unstoppable. She led us to our fifth consecutive national championship and was named the tournament MVP.

That story is a perfect example of the importance of advisors and the importance of letting go of our egos for the greater good of the team. That day, we won a championship in great part because of an engineer reinventing himself as a basketball statistician and a head coach who listened.[4]

LESSONS FROM MY YODAS

Here are my top lessons gleaned from my mentors, which have transformed my coaching, communication, and management approach both personally and within our program. These invaluable lessons have had a remarkable and positive impact on our communication dynamics, significantly improving player preparation, reducing misunderstandings, and fostering stronger collaboration among our coaching staff.

1. To Enhance Coaching Effectiveness and Unity

- Share practice plans with the team in advance, either in person, on a whiteboard, or digitally. This allows them to mentally prepare and be fully engaged when practice begins.
- Require your assistant coaches to share with you all feedback they intend to give a player before they initiate a conversation with them. This practice promotes collaboration and ensures that you are on the same page, leading to a more cohesive approach for the players.
- During games, have one assistant take note of every idea, feedback, or comment you make. These can be reviewed after the game.
- During games, have the assistants give personal feedback to players so that you do not turn your head towards the bench and miss the play. Your job is to manage the game. If you must talk to a player, have an empty chair beside you for them to sit in so you can talk while still watching the game. After the game, have each assistant share the individual feedback that was given so that you can continue to manage your players cohesively.

2. To Increase Communication and Satisfaction

- When scheduling a meeting with a player or coach, clearly state the topic in the text, email, or verbal communication. This gives them time to process and prepare, eliminating unnecessary stress caused by vague requests like "Can you come see me in the office?" The same can be asked of players, so you can prepare effectively for any meeting they request.
- If you anticipate that a discussion may be difficult or hard for a player to hear, consider offering the option for them

to bring a trusted teammate along. This allows for additional support and helps diffuse any potential for them to feel blindsided or overwhelmed.

- Refrain from discussing game underperformances with players through text or email. These forms of communication can easily be misinterpreted, leading to misunderstandings and potential damage. Wait for the opportunity to have a face-to-face conversation instead.

3. To Better Manage a Team Off-Court

- Never make impulsive decisions, such as cutting a player or imposing penalties, on the same day an incident occurs. Instead, inform the player that consequences will be discussed the following day. This provides time for reflection and ensures a clear and fair approach.
- Avoid lengthy meetings immediately after games. If the team loses, allow time for regrouping, and discuss the game with a fresh perspective the next day. If the team wins, celebrate the victory and then constructively shift focus to the next challenge.
- Recognize that as the leader, the final decision rests with you. External opinions from assistant coaches or mentors should be considered, but ultimately you are fully accountable for the choices made, even if you took the opinion of an assistant and it did not turn out well.

4. To Become a Better Person

- Increase your self-awareness through mentorship. A mentor can help you gain deeper insights into your strengths, weaknesses, and blind spots. Allow a mentor to coach you.
- Ask your mentors to share their experiences of overcoming challenges. Listening to them allows you to realize that difficult management situations are present in

everyone's career. Their stories hold a wealth of wisdom and can help you develop resilience and navigate setbacks.

- Embrace and be open to last-minute changes. This adaptability is key to evolving as a leader in a dynamic environment. Coaching is not a routine job that can be scripted ahead of time.

- Seek balance. Learn when to recharge and when to let go. During the season, I adopt a six-to-one cadence (six days of work to one day off a week). Sometimes this means 14- to 16-hour workdays, but the complete 24 hours off—unplugged—reserved for play and for family is really invigorating and keeps me balanced. During the competitive season, I typically work 80–90 hours per week. In the off-season, I work fewer hours, aiming for around 30 hours per week, and take several days to rest. Purposely understanding and creating this space for refueling also keeps me balanced over the years.

CHAPTER 7

Inspiring Through Metaphor

"The mediocre teacher tells. The good teacher explains. The superior teacher demonstrates. The great teacher inspires."

—WILLIAM ARTHUR WARD

When I created a plan for the Lancers at the end of my first season, my vision was clear: we would win our first championship in five years. In the off-season between my fourth and fifth seasons, coming off a heartbreaking loss followed by losing two starters, my faith in my leadership and vision to win a championship had faltered. Feeling I had been the limiting factor, I had begun the tough journey to work on myself as a leader that summer. Now, I had mentors and an assistant coach I trusted. It was time to step up as head coach and lead my team, no matter the odds that seemed stacked against us. The first step: reinspiring them to believe in our vision even though our team was weaker.

This was not a small task: it seemed that the closer we got to our goal, the more afraid of failure I became. It affected our team cohesion and operation. The added blow of our two best scorers opting not to return only heightened it. It felt like the program was, figuratively, in the midst of a survival emergency. I knew I was responsible for finding a way to manage our fear and to focus back on the goal.

That summer, I read the book *Deep Survival: Who Lives, Who Dies, and Why* by Laurence Gonzales, which includes a description of what F-18 pilots go through to land on a ship at sea. The tremendous risk involved has the potential to cause overwhelming stress and anxiety in the moment. A tactic must be put in place to reduce the tension in do-or-die moments because, as Gonzales puts it, "Fear is good. Too much is not." To lighten the weight of the task at hand, the F-18 pilots use nonsense vocabulary that only they can understand. The pilots are taught to "grab the towel rack" and ensure "the beer cans are down" in place of naming the crucial emergency manoeuvre required. This tactic has two major objectives: first, it occupies the brain on the task at hand and distracts from potential panic by using playfulness to keep the person engaged in what is happening around them. Only the two people meant to get the meaning get it. The insider language increases a sense of connection and cohesion for these high-performing pilots.

Inspired by Gonzales's book, the thought crossed my mind to look for a symbolic metaphor that could reinspire my entire team. I wanted to shift the team's focus from the challenges we had been facing to a renewed emphasis on the immediate tasks and the small steps necessary to reach our goal. I looked to other fields and disciplines, visualizations, and stories that would parallel our journey to winning a championship.

CLIMBING EVEREST

That's when the concept of climbing started to take shape in my mind. In my fifth year of coaching the Lancers, the theme suddenly clicked—our journey to peak performance in sports was like summiting a mountain. We weren't just preparing for any challenge; we were going to climb Mount Everest. Everest is not only the most talked-about, it is also the most difficult mountain to climb. It requires strength and an incredible amount of focused effort to accomplish, which clearly paralleled the journey of winning a national championship. We had our sights set on achieving something once deemed impossible, which many had not dared to undertake and conquer. This was going to be *our* story.

As a coaching staff, we created a poster of the summit of Mount Everest and posted it in the team room as a visual reminder of where we were headed. We marked the actual hiking trail and the different altitudes of all the camps (stops to acclimatize and rest along the way) and explained the course we were going to take. The image of climbing our Everest gave the team a sense of purpose and helped us move on from grieving the loss of our two best players. It shifted our focus and made us feel in control of our destiny. It helped develop our own team identity, journey, and jargon. For example, during playoffs, we would not talk about winning the quarter-finals; we talked about getting from base camp to camp one. We didn't talk about winning the national championship, we talked about summiting. Copying the idea used by the F-18 air force pilots, we changed our entire vocabulary. We made a plan akin to climbing the trail along the north face because, even though it is the most travelled, it has the reputation of being the most unpredictable in terms of conditions, and we knew playoffs could be messy. This was our new direction: to reach the top of that peak. And the steps to our first national championship were clear. It was well documented how we could summit Mount Everest:

- A thorough training, fitness, and cardio base in the off-season
- An early arrival to base camp for rehearsal, allowing us to adjust to the altitude and weather conditions
- A series of treacherous passages, some harder than others, to get from base camp to camp one, two, three, four, and finally the summit
- Great Sherpas and team performance through each of the rehearsed hikes
- An understanding of the specific climbing material, lingo, and the roles of each climber
- Previous climbing experience was a bonus to successfully reach the summit
- We may lose some climbers along the way, but the expedition would continue as a team

I cannot emphasize enough how beneficial this strategy ended up being to our team. Everyone bought into the expedition, and our stress level decreased. Although we failed to summit that season, we successfully made it all the way to camp four, the national final. Were we disappointed not to reach our goal of a championship in five years? Yes, but going from a place where I had feared that our vision was lost to getting all the way to the championship game in one season was a massive achievement. In the team room after the loss, I said, "We had to learn to climb before we can learn to summit. We'll see that peak next year." The truth is, if we didn't have that plan behind us, we would not have achieved as high a finish. In the end, whether or not we ended up winning it all in five or six years didn't really matter. We were now mountain climbers.

DRAW FROM ADVERSITY

The following season, year six, my team was so motivated to summit, the way we spoke to each other used more climbing lingo as the season went on. We would talk about preparing ourselves for the potential storms out on the mountains that we couldn't predict or how we were all hooked together by a rope and if one falls, we must hold her and reel her back up. It became clear that the metaphor had truly taken hold during an interview with the media after a playoff game. When asked about how we achieved our goal, our team captain Emily Abbott said enthusiastically, "Sometimes when you climb, there's going to be storms and winds and ice pellets. You never know when the weather can change or what the mountain has in store for you. But in the middle of the storm, we must keep our eyes on the Sherpa ahead of us and hold each other tied with the rope that links us. If one of us falls, we all fall. So, we stayed the course." I smiled when I heard that and will always cherish that moment. I don't know what any outsider thought about this answer, but I knew she was deeply committed to the vision of summiting. She had answered the question with all the lingo that we had been using all year, pretty much oblivious that no one else would understand as deeply as we did.

That year we went one notch further. In the face of our city's struggling economy, we had pushed ourselves to practise and play with unwavering determination. We believed that our resilience could serve as a powerful source of inspiration for our community. If people knew the objective we were striving for, despite the challenges of losing and not receiving the respect we deserved as a program, it might encourage them to persevere in their own lives and situations, even in the smallest of ways. While many felt ashamed of our city, we had intentionally purchased new warm-up shirts adorned with the word *WINDSOR* across the back. During tough times on the court, we would motivate each other by remembering that our city was enduring even more difficult circumstances, so quitting was not an option. We had to find a way to prevail and win. Through our vision of raising our program from the ashes, we also wanted to lift up our community. If we could resurrect our program, Windsor, too, could be revived.

In year six, we won our first national championship. It was a moment of pure magic, an unforgettable experience that will forever be etched in the memories of everyone present. The stage was set, the home court advantage was ours, and we were ready to take on the formidable University of Saskatchewan, led by their well-known head coach. The city had come alive, rallying behind our team, and the energy was palpable. The stands were overflowing, and over 100,000 viewers tuned in to watch us on national TV, as we made history as women's basketball players and coaches. Our journey had begun six years earlier and had been nothing short of inspiring, having gone from the bottom of the pack to the top. The Windsor community had taken immense pride in our success, and the outpouring of support was staggering. We had to isolate our players in a hotel to ensure that they remained focused, as fans and well-wishers clamoured for our attention. Even with a security guard stationed outside my office, fans still found ways to reach me, and their unwavering support was both incredible and overwhelming. I will never forget the grandmother of one of my players, who reached out to touch me, saying that it felt like she had touched Jesus. Equally surprising, another fan found my home address and knocked on the door to give me a hug.

When we lifted the championship trophy over our heads, we knew that we had achieved something truly remarkable not only in sport but for our city. It was a moment of pure, unbridled joy, and the tears of countless fans in the stands, many who had never met us before, were a testament to the impact that our success had had on the Windsor, which later recognized our contribution by giving us the symbolic keys to the city.

The decision to use metaphors to motivate and focus our group was further strengthened that summer when I was watching the 2011 FIFA Women's World Cup, and Japan's head coach Norio Sasaki. If you recall, 2011 was the year Japan was hit with a horrific natural disaster. In March, more than 15,000 people were left dead after the country was devastated by an earthquake-triggered tsunami and subsequent nuclear meltdown. The Japanese women's team was not favoured to win the tournament. Yet, against all odds, the team upset host nation Germany, then Sweden, and then the United States, besting them 3–1 in a dramatic penalty shootout, ultimately winning the 2011 FIFA World Cup.

Norio Sasaki explained how he drew inspiration from the perseverance of the tsunami survivors to motivate his team. Prior to the final, he showed images of the devastation back home to his group of players, reminding them that if their country could get through this, his team could get past the USA. Sasaki believed that the courage of every Japanese person exhibited in this time of peril could be reproduced on the soccer field, and he had the players keep this in mind while playing. He explained,

> I felt it was our responsibility to cheer up the country and encourage our people through our football at least. At the moment of victory, I was observing the whole scene thinking this was like a dream. I thought how proud and happy the people back home would be. We are still recovering from the disaster. There were so many victims in the area that was devastated. Even little things like a win can give people courage and hope.

Before boarding the flight back home from Germany, team captain Homare Sawa said, "I have to dedicate this win to the people who suffered the disaster."

Pulling inspiration from previous experiences or strong metaphors can be very powerful. Motivation does not always need to be drawn from dark situations such as a natural disaster or an economic crisis, but it does require some element of creativity. The use of metaphors as a tool has the ability to motivate through powerful visualization and insider connections among team members. I remember talking to a colleague in our league about the importance of inspiring our athletes, following her complaint that players were not motivated enough to schedule individual training sessions. She exclaimed, "It's not my job to motivate them!" I cannot emphasize enough that it absolutely *is* the coach's job to motivate players. In my opinion and observation of the best leaders, I have found that the ability to motivate is a key leadership ingredient in building momentum to achieve the vision. It can even uplift people to achieve better results than anticipated. It can make a difference between merely competing and winning it all.

As for us in Windsor, the players spent the summer designing a special Mount Everest shirt with their signatures. It read, "Who knew Mount Everest was in Windsor?" This metaphor turned out to be so useful that each year we won a national championship, we chose a different peak to summit.

CHAPTER 8

Top Ten Lessons Learned from Coaching

"Life will give you whatever experience is most helpful for the evolution of your consciousness."

—ECKHART TOLLE

In the 1950s, long-distance swimmer Florence Chadwick was one of the few women practising the sport seriously. In 1952, Florence set a goal to swim from Catalina Island to the California coast: 26 miles in cold and rough ocean waters. As she began, she was accompanied by her mom in a small boat watching for sharks. After about 16 hours, Florence felt extremely tired and began to doubt her ability to complete her goal. She asked her mother to be pulled out. As she sat in the boat, she was astonished to find out that she had stopped swimming just one mile short of her destination. She told the reporters that she didn't want to make excuses, but the fog was so thick she couldn't see the coastline. "If I could have seen the shore, I would have kept going" is all the swimmer could offer. Like most people, Chadwick gave up on her journey not knowing just how close she was to reaching her goal because she could not *see* it.

Two months later, she tried again. Unfortunately, the same thick fog set in, and the coastline had once again disappeared from her sight, but this time, she succeeded! While focusing on each of her strokes, one at a time, she explained that she kept a mental picture of the shoreline in her mind all through her swim. The shoreline, the end goal, had become her vision.

Successful people keep their eyes on the shore and not on the distractions. They keep their heads above water and keep breathing regularly even when they feel overwhelmed. The experience I have acquired through keeping my eyes on our vision is invaluable. I have selected ten lessons that were transformative for me as a coach.

> ## TIME-OUT
> Reflection is an important learning pathway in coaching. Many coaches engage in superficial and simplistic reflections; however, coaching effectiveness requires deeper critical reflection, which takes time, commitment, and practice. Reflection helps increase self-awareness and is a skill one must improve in order to become a better coach. His principle applies equally to any leadership role, whether it's parents, managers, or team leaders.[1]

1. The Struggle Is Real

No one likes to be uncomfortable. Leading an organization or a group of people can feel, at times, as if we are swimming in cold water surrounded by sharks and thick fog. Whether suffering through physical or emotional pain, unless tended to, it can cripple us. Holding on to past mistakes or fearing potential failure can eventually be debilitating.

The solution to this is to see pain, failure, and unsettling experiences as great teachers and to work to understand those lessons. As such, we must lean in, listen, seek, and find out what opportunity to heal or adjust our life has been set before us. Pain does not call for resistance or complaining. It is an open path to transformation and betterment. Pain is a wake-up call, and when answered properly, it can be our greatest teacher.

2. Next Play

In the face of adversity, uncertainty or failure, emotions do not define us; they are temporary responses to situations. Emotions are transient, meaning they come and go, sometimes quite irrationally. They are also an important part of our growth process. Emotions are meant to move us forward, not backwards. We need to make room to work through them, and we can learn to let them pass through us via some simple techniques such as breathing exercisesor a key word to repeat. The phrase 'next play' is the mantra that I repeat whenever I find myself in such situations.

In the midst of a game, controlling emotions is key because they can steal momentum or be the catalyst for panic and chaos. We need to be able to keep going, to move ahead to the next play. As leaders, controlling and letting go of our emotions is necessary in order to clearly communicate directions, offer feedback, set the tone for confidence, and move forward.

Emotions are part of every leader's reality, part of any sports game, and obviously part of everyone's life. Our experiences are filled with ups and downs, just like the waves of an ocean. During a crisis moment, leaders need to stay the course, stand firm, sail through the emotions, keep their direction clear and their eyes on the destination. When you aren't feeling at your best, that "next play" mentality will keep you driving forward. It encourages leaving setbacks behind and staying committed to the task at hand. When the storm passes, you will still be standing tall—leading and directing.

3. One Voice Is Harmony

The concept of one voice is something my assistant coach Tom Foster came up with after our fourth season. We had lost the bronze medal at the national championship, in part because of the chaos of everyone yelling different instructions from the bench. In heated moments, only the voice of the head coach should be heard.

This doesn't mean that players and assistants are not consulted, do not share their opinions, or do not have a say. In fact, the complete opposite is true. Players and coaches are encouraged to chime in. Collaboration and differences of opinion are welcomed. One voice means that as the stakes get higher, in critical moments, space and quiet are needed for the head coach to take everything into consideration and then make the right decision alone. In those moments, a one voice approach makes all the difference in avoiding confusion. It unites the coaching staff and the team, and it prevents doubt from creeping into the leader's mind. More important than chipping in with a suggestion or being "right" or "wrong" when the game is on the line, what is needed is one voice with clear direction.

4. Preparation Is Confidence

The Navy SEALs have a saying: "Under pressure, you don't rise to the occasion, you sink to the level of your training." Thorough preparation and repetition ensure undeniable confidence in what they execute under pressure. If they aren't successful in repeating procedures for hours during training, the message is clear: they won't be successful when it counts.

In 2018, I was sitting in the office of the future NBA championship coach (then head coach of the Toronto Raptors) Nick Nurse, who repeated the same thing. Sitting behind his desk with blues playing in the background, he took a dry-erase marker and wrote on his board "ATOs" (what you run after a time-out), "EOQs" (at the end of the quarter), and "EOGs" (at the end of the game). He explained, "Those must be prepared and repped [repeated] over and over. Under pressure, if you did not practise those, your team will likely fail."

Since that day, I created a cheat sheet that I carry in my pocket for heated in-game decision. It contains the plays we have rehearsed many times for end-of-game and high-pressure situations. Nothing new is introduced when we are under pressure in a game. In the heat of the moment, I don't get distracted by pressure but rather think tactically and follow the procedures we've prepared with the team for specific situations. Even breathing to cool down or recentre ourselves is rehearsed. I have come to see the benefit of creating a similar list for my life. How do I want to react when someone makes a rude comment, or I experience sadness or frustration? This way, the direction to take remains clear, and the execution of the desired behaviour is successful.

5. Less Is More

The adage "You cannot overprepare" is false. This may seem to be in direct contrast to the previous lesson, but overpreparing, overcoaching, and oversharing information can lead to increased stress and anxiety. Adding extra practice time, lengthy scouting reports, and unnecessary meetings can be detrimental to a team's success and lead to discouragement or a sense of panic. A good leader knows how to reduce stress and instill confidence. This can be achieved by ensuring that players feel confident in their roles and reminding them that the necessary preparation has already been done with excellence and efficiency. Nick Nurse narrowed down his team preparation to four simple points: knowing player personnel, simple offence, simple defence, and end-of-game (EOG) situations rehearsed. The message is clear: keep it simple. It's important for coaches to understand that less is often more. A good leader knows the difference between thorough preparation and obsessiveness. Choosing to focus on what's truly necessary will reduce anxiety and keep the players healthy, while also giving them a genuine sense of confidence and readiness before important games. When in doubt, choose less.

6. Readiness Is Mandatory

Readiness is a non-negotiable because it teaches us to relax and trust in the process of competing. There comes a point when control of the outcomes must be relinquished from coaches over to players. This may create a sense of helplessness, as coaches no longer have control. At Windsor, we made a pact that, whether we felt ready or not, we lead practices before important games with an undeniable faith that we are ready. As leaders, we control our doubts by choosing to believe that what we have done is enough and that our preparation is thorough. Prior to a game, we need to let go of control and let the game unfold.

A few seconds before entering the team room during our third national championship final, I felt nervous and underprepared. Three games in three days allowed for little sleep and not enough time to strategically prepare for our opponents. Holding strong to this rule, I raised my hand forward, and the assistant coaches did the same for a little coach cheer. "We are ready," I said, and everyone nodded. It didn't matter how we felt. Since readiness is mandatory, I opted that we focus on ourselves. We won our third national title that day.

7. Help Is Non-negotiable

Research shows that mentoring is key to success. While mentors are one way to get help, they are not the only way. Peer relationships, players' input, books, movies, successful leaders in other fields, research—the idea is to learn from any source available. It is not possible to transform a program, lead successfully, or influence others all alone. There are times we need to be willing to let someone else who is more capable at a task take the lead. Asking for help is a great cure for our own ego and a great way to share championships with a team of people who, most often, will become friends rather than just colleagues.

8. Adaptability Is Key

Ask yourself, on the following spectrum, where do you think an effective leader should be placed?

Most of us would think that an effective coach would fall somewhere in the middle.

Research on transformational leadership stipulates that this is not the case. Rather, successful leaders must be able to display behaviours that can be found anywhere on the spectrum at any given time, depending on the situation. This means being adaptable and perceptive. What I came to understand is that the best leaders are able to display the appropriate characteristic at the appropriate time in any specific situation. This is how an effective leader should be:

It is easy to change the words at each end of the spectrum for different personal characteristics pertaining to leadership (benevolent or dictator, asking or telling, demanding or suggesting, easygoing or laying down the law, etc.). It is challenging, yet necessary, to become adept at each of these spectrums. Embodying all of the behaviours that each contains and knowing when to display each of them are the keys to successful leadership. Surround yourself with mentors who can point to areas of leadership weakness and help you fill your spectrum fully.

9. Growth Is Necessary

If we do not like where the team is going, we need to change our methods or we need to change ourselves. To be successful in business, or in any endeavour for that matter, there needs to be an investment in people. Author Simon Sinek argues that Starbucks crafted a vision to create not just exceptional coffee but also a space for people to hang out. Discussions and meetings, advising and counselling happened in the coffee shops, which offered customers the opportunity to foster their individual growth. The intention was that offering this space would grow the business as people connected. "The coffee was incidental," as Sinek explains. Yes, Starbucks displays revenues of billions of dollars a year.

Being a leader automatically involves managing people, motivating troops to achieve results, manoeuvring through difficult situations, and learning how to set a clear and unified direction. Leaders must welcome personal growth, or they will not survive. There is a powerful saying related to this: "The team usually improves right after the leader does." Overcoming challenges and setbacks can be gruelling, and receiving feedback, positive or negative, can be tough. But the journey of personal growth and transformation is the most rewarding one that I have ever embarked on. It has allowed me to become a better leader and ultimately a better human being. The key is to embrace change and let go of the past. We must be willing to reinvent ourselves, seek self-awareness, and be open to feedback and guidance from mentors and counsellors. It is not always easy, but the internal desire to improve is a gift that we all possess.

In order to reach success as a leader and coach, I first had to transform myself. I learned that I could not expect to change an entire team culture without being part of the change myself. Basketball was incidental.

10. The End Is Inevitable

Ancient legends tell of the magical phoenix, which has radiant colours of reds and yellows and is said to live for hundreds of years before it dies by bursting into flames. When the phoenix felt its end coming, it would build a nest, set it on fire, flap its wings to fan the fire, and burn in the flames. While it was being reduced to ashes and the fire was cooling down, a chick would be reborn from the ashes to start a new, long life. The phoenix symbolizes the cycle of life, death, and resurrection, and it is a powerful symbol of personal transformation. The end of something great can be a daunting prospect for anyone. But just like the mythical phoenix, we, too, can rise from the ashes of our past to create a new, stronger version of ourselves.

As a coach, I have witnessed the power of embracing the phoenix within. As leaders, we must recognize that the world is constantly evolving, and we must adapt to stay relevant. We must be willing to revamp our strategies, philosophies, and methods to become stronger leaders. We must also accept that people and situations come and go in our lives, and that grieving is a normal part of the process.

In the end, closing one chapter of our lives brings opportunities for new beginnings. The end is inevitable, but personal transformation is the gift of life.

QUARTER BREAK

Four Keys to Elevating your Leadership

1. **EXPECT CRISES.** As a leader, you will inevitably face challenges. It's not a matter of if but when. By expecting crises, you prepare yourself and your team to handle them with grace and ease, rather than being emotionally drained by them.

2. **FALL FORWARD.** Setbacks are a part of the journey to success. Don't let them hold you back. Embrace them, learn from them, and find opportunities to grow stronger. Setbacks offer new perspectives and the potential to move forward stronger.

3. **SEEK YOUR YODA.** Feedback is crucial to growth. Look for mentors who have diverse life experiences and who can help you develop as a coach. Be open to criticism, and engage in self-analysis. Don't let pride hold you back from changing your approach and improving yourself.

4. **BECOME A BETTER PERSON.** A leader's journey is never complete. The team improves as the leader does. Observe yourself and practise deep self-reflection. As you overcome your own limitations, you'll be better equipped to help your team overcome theirs.

COACH INSIGHT: Seek anonymous feedback. It may be uncomfortable at first, but the rewards are worth it. Many times I have sought anonymous feedback through a survey.

With the right mindset, I discovered new ways to grow and transform myself as a leader and a person.

LOOK AHEAD TO THE THIRD QUARTER

The journey to success is more like a winding road than a straight line. Along the way, we inevitably face extended periods of drought and doubt. Keep reading to learn how to prepare and build grit.

THIRD QUARTER

The Grind

"Greatness is sifted through the grind, therefore don't despise the hard work now for surely it will be worth it in the end."

—SANJO JENDAYI

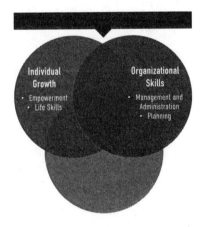

Standing as a national champion, the victory is more than a triumph; it's a realization of a dream and vision passionately pursued for years. The real reward is in having endured the relentless grind that led you there. So, embrace the grind, because becoming a champion isn't in the win; it's in the path that made every ounce of effort worthwhile: pushing, believing, and remembering the effort, passion, and dedication you invested in the journey. It's about the resilience built through adversity, the unity formed with others on the same path, and the growth that transformed you. It's a reflection of the maturity developed, the bonds forged with lifelong friends, and the culture created within yourself and the team. What sets champions apart is their unwavering commitment to this journey and their ability to overcome the grind victoriously.

Our research model identified two key higher-order categories essential for overcoming the grind. The first, individual growth, emphasizes the personalized attention that keeps players focused and committed to the team's shared goal. The second, organizational skills, highlights that successful leaders are well organized and embrace the daily administrative responsibilities that extend beyond coaching.

CHAPTER 9

Building Culture for the Grind

"You don't sell the culture; you catch it."
—DR. WADE GILBERT

One of my all-time sources of inspiration on winning is the New Zealand national men's rugby team, known as the All Blacks, considered by many expert researchers as the best sporting organization in the world. Even to a non-rugby fan, the mere mention of the All Blacks may evoke a distinct image of the team doing a pre-game chant and choreographed dance called the Haka. Over the course of their hundred-year existence, the All Blacks have maintained a winning percentage over 75 percent, boasting three Rugby World Cup titles and a runner-up finish. The All Blacks secured their world championship victories on home turf in 1987, 2011, and once more in 2015, achieving the historic feat of winning consecutive Rugby World Cups, a feat no other nation has ever achieved. This makes them the most successful elite sports team of the past century. However, back in 2003, the All Blacks had fallen from grace as the world's premier rugby team. New Zealand lost to Australia in the semi-finals, which put the team in the lowest rank in the club's history. The All Blacks were going through a rough period, one that is often called "the grind" in sport.

After a time working through the grind, the All Blacks needed a comeback, and newly appointed coaches Graham Henry and Wayne Smith began to rebuild the team from the inside out by powerfully redirecting and rebranding the team's overall culture. In their minds, the grind had to be overcome through an entire revamping of the organization's demeanour, standards, and expectations, not just a winning record. They did not immediately address performance, physical fitness, or on-field talent; instead, they aimed at changing the players' behaviours off the field first. The coaches felt that each All Black needed to dig deeper and change his own mindset to engineer a positive transformation at the team level. The All Blacks became the pioneers of the concept of team culture now so prevalently discussed in sports and business organizations.

The All Blacks adopted the motto "better people make better All Blacks." The team shifted focus onto each athlete's character, mindset and growth by holding him to higher personal standards off the field. Their five-point character plan developed for engineering this culture shift had nothing to do with rugby and everything to do with becoming better human beings.

1. Sweep the Shed

Before leaving the dressing room at the end of the game, all players tidy up after themselves. This act of humility ensures that the players remain grounded as they reach superstardom.

2. Follow the Spearhead

In the Māori culture of New Zealand, the spearhead symbolizes the extended family. The All Blacks added character to the player recruitment criteria. New players have to meet a set of personal standards. Many of New Zealand's most promising players never wore the black jersey because their inclusion would have threatened the All Blacks family. "No dickheads" became the team mantra.

3. Champions Do Extra

This is a philosophy that focuses on each player's own on-field performance and off-field personal growth and learning. It means finding incremental ways to do more: one more rep in the gym, one more sprint on the field. This concept of "better people make better All Blacks" spills over to make them better citizens, doctors, teachers, coaches, businessmen, fathers, brothers, and friends—because they do extra.

4. Keep a Blue Head

The All Blacks put a lot of emphasis on emotional control. The team's mental skills consultant, Ceri Evans, explains that symbolically, a red head is comparable to choking: being overwhelmed, panicked, and ineffective. On the other hand, a blue head is optimal performing, on task, focused, and in the zone. They use actions, keywords, or visual cues as indicators to switch from red to blue, which enables players to perform under pressure with clarity and accuracy.

5. Leave the Jersey in a Better Place

An All Black player is a role model to children in his country and sees his role as embodying a higher purpose rather than solely playing rugby. The All Blacks are tasked with representing those who have come before them and with creating a legacy for those who will follow. When they retire, they must leave the program bettered by their participation.[1]

The All Blacks were right to invest in a character plan first. The way their players had been behaving off the field was not conducive to a winning program. Those men did not possess the character traits that could get them through the grind of a tough season or even tough sections of a game. After the establishment of the new culture, the transformation propelled the team to an 85 percent winning percentage from 2004 to 2011. The impact of the All-Blacks' work on prioritizing team culture deepened my understanding of why teams are successful. It redirected their team towards winning. The All Blacks are considered the best rugby nation in the world and are regarded by some as the greatest sports organization of all time. Their success is the reason I travelled to New Zealand in 2019 to meet them, learn from them, and work with them.

After spending time with them and reflecting on my own journey of creating our championship program, it became even more apparent that it was team culture that promoted a sense of unity and purpose strong enough to lift both our Lancer team and the All Blacks to success. Coach Wayne Smith and I discussed how important team culture was when our organizations faced challenges and difficulties. Our respective cultures fought against mediocrity, bad habits, and even helped push away potential burnouts by giving each member a sense of belonging and purpose. We agreed that a strong culture can't simply be announced; it requires the continual daily effort of every member, first and foremost initiated and upheld by the leader—the coach. Building our cultures was a continuous process that required observation and reflection, analysis of gaps and proficiencies, setting new standards, creating an environment for growth, and providing accountability. Building a team culture has very little to do with the direct coaching of athletes and a lot more to do with managing personalities, people, expectations, and the environment, as well as being clear about our values. By linking our values and standards to our vision, by fostering a growth mindset, and by keeping everyone accountable—that is how we built the championship cultures that allowed us to climb to the tops of our respective sports. Figure 6 details the steps I used to build a deliberate culture within the Lancers organization. We have not only been successful on the court, but we have also graduated all of our athletes, produced seven professional players and one Olympian, and empowered three assistants to become full-time head coaches at other universities during a span of six years.

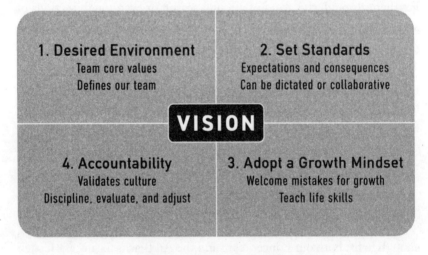

Figure 6: Building Team Culture

STEP 1: DESIRED ENVIRONMENT

In the mid-2000s, when we began transforming the Windsor Lancers program, the term *team culture* wasn't yet popular. As coaches, we discussed the environment we wanted in the form of key behaviours that we wanted to change. The top-down approach of dictating rules from the start of the season allowed us to outline the culture we had in mind. However, we quickly realized that this approach was very restrictive for the players. Players challenged us constantly and broke the rules, which was a harsh leadership lesson.

One such lesson happened in my first year of coaching. We were playing an away game and got crushed badly. After the game, my assistant coach Tom and I went back to the hotel lobby to have a serious talk about what had gone wrong. Little did we know, a group of our players, all dressed up, were headed to the bar! And they were so excited about it that they didn't even notice us standing there.

When we went to put a stop to their plans, these players were not having it. They started dropping F-bombs and even threatened to quit the team. The veterans and captains demanded a meeting with coaches and insisted that if they couldn't go out and drink, neither could we (pointing to the wineglasses in front of us). They said if they had a curfew, we should, too, and if they couldn't eat junk food, then we couldn't either. The one-way lecture from my captain went on for quite a while.

We tried to explain to them that these rules were in place to help them perform better, but they could not accept that the rules for coaches were different. After a long and heated discussion, they finally agreed to comply with most of the rules. But it was a nightmare to enforce them. These players constantly challenged my authority. We had to suspend players, reprimand the team, deal with angry parents, and even had to remove players from the roster. But we made it through and can now have some good laughs about it. It's all part of the wild ride that comes with coaching a team, I suppose.

Over the years, I've learned a better approach is to find players who *want* to operate in the environment we have in mind, in the same way that I had discovered how important it was to build a roster of players who have bought into our team vision. When I first started coaching, I had to be strict and inflexible to get the team in line. But as we started recruiting our own players, we were able to explain our expectations upfront, so athletes could commit to them before joining the team and decline an offer if they did not like the parameters. Then we started involving players in the conversation, asking for their input on what they wanted our environment to be. Eventually, we stopped using words like *rules* and instead talked about *expectations, standards, non-negotiables,* and *values.* This small change had a big impact: it felt less imposing and restrictive to the players, and they were compelled to willingly conduct themselves in ways we collectively deemed acceptable.

It took time, but eventually the message was received. It was not until year three that we stopped *policing* players and could finally *manage* them. They bought into our team standards effortlessly. When our veteran players expressed a desire for more involvement, we transformed our team values into a concise and motivational document called "The Lancer Way" (Figure 7). To create it, I conducted an exercise where each player wrote down what they believed our Lancer culture represented. We compiled the ideas into a master sheet, labelled each idea, and organized them into four key categories. This document became a powerful representation of our team's values, providing clarity and direction for our program. As we'll see later, having clearly defined values makes it easier to make tough decisions when necessary.

TIME-OUT

In one case study, athletes and a mental performance consultant created a "team covenant" that guided how the team acted and behaved both inside and outside of sport. The athletes adhered to the covenant because they were a big part of its creation.[2]

The Lancer Way

EXCELLENCE

We train to get excellent results.

We learn to deal with pressure, to compete, to perform, to overcome, and to win. We don't cut corners, we are accountable, we work the hardest of any teams, and we perform. We also understand that excellence is not perfection. It's the maximum we can give, and we give it.

GROWTH

We accept being uncomfortable because we want to grow.

We agree to be pushed beyond our comfort zone. We seek to be uncomfortable. We understand that our struggle is a mirror of what we need to work on. We want to grow our basketball skills, as performers, and personally. We want to sort ourselves out on the floor and in life.

STRENGTH

We are women of character and physical strength.

We are women who possess grit and strength of character. We are resilient and perseverant. This is significant because we need to stand strong on the wood court and in society. We are leaders and role models for character and physical strength. We embody strength and agree to use it to stand out above the crowd by bettering ourselves and communities in all areas of life.

FAMILY

We are family.

We are welcoming of everyone independent of culture, religion, ethnicity, and sexual orientation. We engage with the fans, recruits, parents, and community. We are truthful and honest with each other because we operate with respect and integrity. We have each other's backs and will do anything to protect our family. With basketball matters, our basketball family comes first.

Figure 7: The Lancer Way

STEP 2: SETTING STANDARDS

The Lancer Way was a visual tool to remind us what we wanted our environment to be. After defining our desired environment, we proceeded to elevate our standards across various aspects of our on-court expectations. This encompassed practices, games, travels, physical and mental fitness, as well as performance benchmarks. Rather than imposing strict rules, we found that players responded much better when presented with these elevated standards upfront.

However, it is not always a walk in the park to have players buy in. In the fall of 2010, first-year player Jocelyn LaRocque came to my office feeling frustrated and upset. She was training and practising hard, but she wasn't getting much playing time. I told her that hard work was an expectation, not a differentiating factor in playing time. Can you note the difference? For the Lancers, practising hard, going to all weight training sessions, never missing a practice, giving 100 percent effort, knowing all the plays, and doing it with a great attitude does not buy playing time. Performance on game day does. You may think, "What if a player doesn't show up to all practices, lacks effort, but performs when games come around?" This is not possible because this player would not be part of our team. I asked Jocelyn, "Who on the team does not work hard?" and her answer was "no one." I replied, "Keep working hard, and shift your focus to finding ways to improve your performance in practices and in games. That is what gets you playing time."

It was a tough challenge for Jocelyn as she kept struggling with short shifts and playing with fear and pressure. I then explained to her that performing is a skill that can be learned, improved, and mastered. She needed to focus on how to master performing in her role, and she took this head-on. Jocelyn became one of only two players to win all five championships. In her final year, she was still one of the hardest-working athletes, now a starter on the team—and yes, a great performer. Just to show how tough of a performer she became, she had severe food poisoning at her last national championship appearance. The illness was so severe that she couldn't keep any food down and had to stay back at the hotel during our semi-final game. However, refusing to let her career end on that note, she relied on Pedialyte for sustenance and courageously returned to play the next day for the final game. She started, scored, and defended as she normally would, helping push the team towards victory. After a great performance and our fifth national championship, Jocelyn could not stay to celebrate; she returned immediately to her hotel room, still unwell. Jocelyn's ability to perform was impressive and nothing short of a full embodiment of having bought in to our philosophy of performance. It allowed her to bring forth a performance that none of us expected given her extreme sickness.

STEP 3: ADOPTING A GROWTH MINDSET

As part of our Lancer program, we defined growth as accepting that being uncomfortable at times is necessary and must be welcomed. Our viewpoint on growth is based on *Mindset: The New Psychology of Success* by Dr. Carol S. Dweck. According to Dweck's research, human beings are either caught in a fixed mindset, meaning they believe their talents and abilities are unchangeable, or they possess a growth mindset, which means they believe their abilities can be developed through hard work and persistence.

To help the team understand Dr. Dweck's concepts of fixed and growth mindsets, I use the analogy of a runner's lactate threshold graph. In physical performance, the lactate threshold is the point at which lactic acid accumulates in muscles faster than it can be removed, leading to fatigue and decreased performance. This threshold can be determined in a laboratory.

In Figure 8, the lactate threshold (LT) is identified at the point where the graph line begins to move exponentially upwards. Hypothetically, for the use of our metaphor, someone with a fixed mindset would believe that their LT would always remain at that single data point over time. They think they'll always hit the same limit, with no room for improvement. Fixed mindset individuals believe their abilities and potential are static and limited. On the other hand, someone with a growth mindset would believe that the LT, with proper training and effort, can be moved further to the right on the axis confirming that change and progress is possible. They understand that consistent training, during which they gently push themselves past the painful threshold point, can improve their threshold. Individuals with a growth mindset believe their abilities and potential can be developed through hard work, learning, and perseverance.

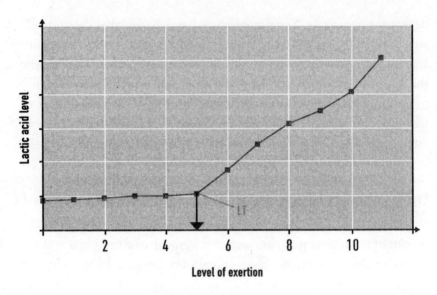

Figure 8: Lactic Acid Threshold in Muscles

We all have the ability with a growth mindset to move our threshold points—whether physical, mental, emotional, or another skill set—with the right approach and training. In certain circumstances, someone might freeze, be scared, become irritated or overwhelmed, and those reactions can be worked on, changed, and improved, as long as a growth mindset is adopted in the face of adversity. Of course, the metaphor is even on point with the fact that continuing to train or push oneself physically beyond the LT point is going to be painful. Similarly, pushing past personal limits, fears, or patterns of reacting to situations and striving for growth will also be uncomfortable. Hence the importance of accepting that being uncomfortable is necessary for personal growth.

In a captivating documentary featuring the All Blacks, a significant statement by Ceri Evans, forensic psychiatrist and mental skills consultant for the team, caught my attention: "If you cannot control your mind, you are of no use to us." This perspective supports Dweck's growth mindset teachings. Learn about yourself *first*; sort yourself out *now*; figure out why you have anxiety, breakdowns, or imbalances *today*. Then you will be a great All Black. While it has been long understood that sports instill valuable life skills, the All Blacks took it a step further. They didn't just invite players to get uncomfortable; they completely inverted the narrative. They prioritize diving into one's emotional and mental realities (and moving past the threshold point), before even aspiring to compete and achieve victory as an athlete. The All Blacks' philosophy reinforces the idea that a solid foundation in self-awareness and emotional balance is crucial for excelling in sports. Challenges don't strengthen character; they reveal it.[3]

Self-evaluation is critical because it reveals the gaps that exist in everyone's behaviours and mindsets and calls for a need to grow. This is something that I experienced personally as a coach, and then it was time for my players to do the same. I wanted to create an atmosphere similar to the one I had found—one that encouraged them to seek improvement personally and in their sporting careers. To do this, I focused on creating a brave environment, teaching them to be aware of personal thresholds.

Creating a brave and supportive environment is crucial for athletes to feel comfortable and experience growth. (In contrast to a safe space, brave spaces accommodate risk and discomfort.) It is risky to push oneself to new heights, and it's essential to have a coach who understands the importance of trust. That's why we always make sure to ask for their permission before we start to put them through high-pressure situations. When they give me permission, we simulate challenges they will face in games, whether physical, mental, emotional, or performance-related. The goal is to help them recognize their own threshold points and learn to keep their composure through it. We encourage them to recognize when they experience a change in their behaviour, mood, or strength. When they hit a threshold point, they can either slow down and stop, or purposefully push themselves a tad bit further. And here's the thing: pushing themselves gently outside a comfort zone is the key to growth. They need to be willing to be uncomfortable in order to grow.

To make it easier, we use colour terms to help players identify their threshold points. Green is feeling great, yellow is feeling a bit uneasy, orange is when they feel they need to start exhibiting self-control, and red is when it has gone too far—they lose their temper, quit, or cry. We do not want them to go there, as it can be counterproductive. By identifying their threshold and pushing themselves carefully into the orange zone, they create an enhanced self-awareness and learn to get back to the yellow and eventually the green zone on their own. With time, they become more resilient, gritty, tough, in shape . . . whatever the point of emphasis may be.

As my coaching career progressed, I found it profoundly gratifying to discover that successful organizations, such as the All Blacks, and influential researchers in other fields, such as Carol Dweck, align closely with our research model. Their approaches underscore the significance of individual growth, which emerged as one of the four key pillars in our study. This concept highlights the essential role of focusing on each person's development and reveals that fostering individual growth involves both life skills development and athlete empowerment. I've always been inspired by a quote from one of the coaches we studied:

> I teach the athletes that there are things you just cannot control, like reacting to referees. I focus on helping them manage their character and emotions, which I believe will benefit them throughout their lives. I draw parallels to the workforce; the skills they learn here are also applicable beyond sports.

Leaders across various fields, including the highly successful university coaches we interviewed, share a common philosophy: they empower and uplift their teams to create positive environments where individuals can acquire essential life skills and build self-confidence. Empowerment in these settings involves valuing each athlete's independence, ideas, and potential, whether they are starters or bench players. Coaches actively seek input from their athletes and encourage their leadership on and off the court. One coach poignantly remarked:

> I work with people, not numbers. I put more effort into developing individuals than in winning titles. Winning a national championship means nothing if, in the following year, six players leave school. Basketball is just a means; the real goal is the development of my athletes.

At the start of my career, I took the concept of individual growth very seriously. When combined with accountability, it became the most effective way to set and maintain high standards, ultimately fostering a strong and positive culture.

THE PAIN OF GRIEF

One of the most difficult things to address in sports is grief. Grief is felt in two main ways in a team setting: deselection and role definition. Players grieve when a friend gets cut or replaced, or when they personally lose game-time minutes or a specific role on the team. At a micro level, there is even a grieving process that takes place when someone is subbed off for making a mistake. When it comes to accepting a role, especially when the player is disappointed in the role assigned, the grieving period is inevitable. What's important to note is that there is growth potential in the way athletes respond to each of these situations.

As part of our culture, we make sure to differentiate the person from the action. We take time to demonstrate how their role on the court may change, but their role as a member of the team remains significant. We also allow them to grieve the loss on their own timeline as we recognize that the process for acceptance varies from person to person.

We tell players that if they decide to continue with their assigned role, they will still be an integral part of the team, but that they must come back without bitterness. For serious cases, if they decide to leave, we give them our blessing and accept their choice. Our experience is that, in most cases, players adapt to their new role, and no issues arise. Being deselected or put through a role change is an incredible personal growth opportunity for developing healthy coping skills, understanding how to let go, and developing resiliency. It also serves to develop the crucial life lesson of differentiating between what they do and who they are. The separation of these concepts is critical to a person's readiness to accept feedback and grow in a healthy way in all facets of skill development, as well as in their personal life.

Because every one of our university-age athletes is still developing, we want them to be hungry for improvement and new skills. Role definition should never put them in a box and categorize them as what they can or cannot do. It is important to remember that players buy into the culture when they feel they have a purpose. As such, we give players with limited skills the chance to work on what they want to improve in practices. For example, we may run a team scrimmage so they can hone skills they hope to eventually use in games. This usually brings about great results. First, it shows them that they may not be ready to attempt these skills in games. Second, it gives us an opportunity to encourage their growth by working together during individual training sessions and summer training. Part of allowing for grief lets players know that change is not permanent or stagnant. Throughout the year, a player can improve and try to earn an expanded role on the team. Acceptance is arguably the one necessary factor in positive self-image, cooperative team culture, and improving individual performance, in any role. The ability to teach growth through grief is unexplored in the coaching world.

STEP 4: ACCOUNTABILITY

Accountability is the glue that binds a team culture together and propels the team towards success. Every day, we have the opportunity to hold ourselves accountable for our actions and decisions and to strive for a better tomorrow. To achieve this with the Lancers, we began by outlining how we would remain accountable to each of our values. Take excellence, for example. Through our collective experience, we discovered that excellence is a combination of hard work and performance sustained over a long period of time. We created a mathematical formula: $€ = t (HW + P)$, where $€$ represents excellence, t represents time, HW represents hard work, and P represents performance. This formula highlights the crucial importance of hard work and performance, as they are both necessary for sustained excellence. These skills set the tone for our culture and give players a practical means to hold themselves accountable.

What does hard work really mean? Hard work is not evaluated based on the amount of sweat or hours of practice, but rather on intention, concentration, organization, preparation, and quality repetition during training. The 10,000-hour rule is the brainchild of renowned psychologist K. Anders Ericsson, who discovered that true expertise is the result of deliberate practice sustained for at least 10,000 hours. I challenge my players to embrace this concept by watching their body language, checking to see if they're truly engaged or just going through the motions. I can tell when they're mindlessly repeating the same drills without really pushing themselves. That's not the kind of hard work we value on our team. Being present and focused on the task is difficult to maintain for a long period of time, but it is the key to deliberate practice.

TIME-OUT

A 1993 paper alluded to the importance of the coach or teacher in facilitating the process of deliberate practice. For example, in the absence of coaches or teachers, they found that subjects usually played rather than practised. Feedback was crucial, and expert performers needed to be taught and corrected when errors occurred. It was also found that a teacher could hinder the development of a student by denying them the proper drills, exercises, and repetitions needed to reach an elite level.[4]

Muscle memory is another important concept that underpins deliberate practice. The electrical signals from our brains to our muscles become stronger the more we repeat a certain action. The more frequently neurons are used to fire a signal using the same pathway, the more myelin wraps around them. This increases the conduction speed of the pathway, which accelerates the electrical current from the brain to the muscle. As a result, the more you repeat an action, the more quickly you'll be able to complete it. The myelination of neural pathways gives athletes their edge, proving the importance of working hard with deliberate focus and concentration. It is almost like physical proof that you've kept yourself accountable. The body shows evidence of the hard work put in.

Accountability is also required off the court. This includes meal preparation on Sundays, studying and keeping up with schoolwork, scheduling routine medical checks as a preventative measure, planning days of rest, meeting with the coach, reviewing videos, and so on. For the players, their routines can be planned down to the smallest details, like when they will eat and when they will nap. They cannot operate in our program and fly by the seat of their pants.

What about performance? You might think the ability to perform comes naturally, but this, too, is a skill that needs to be taught. I accomplish this by bringing in research and information, suggesting videos to watch, and even stretching the players beyond their comfort zones to learn performing skills.

In 2017, everyone was feeling the pressure to win a sixth national championship, and my team experienced some level of anxiety about losing games. So, we teamed up with the Windsor Symphony Orchestra. The maestro himself had actually reached out with a great idea: the Lancers were invited to perform with the orchestra at a series of concerts. And not just any piece, we were going to perform "A Grand, Grand Overture" by Malcolm Arnold, which required us to play some seriously unconventional instruments such as vacuum cleaners. Yes, you read that right. My players were going to "play" these instruments live during three shows over a weekend.

Now I was thrilled about the idea. My players? Not so much. They were terrified. But this was a great teaching moment for them. An opportunity to conquer their fears and practise their performance skills. They nailed it. They performed on cue, turning those vacuums on and off like pros. After each show, they were giggling like little kids on Christmas morning.

The best part is that this experience taught them something invaluable: performance transcends all disciplines. Whether they're playing sports, making art, or interviewing for a job, the performance skill is the same. They have to practise, pay attention to the details, and stay focused—this is where the accountability piece comes in. In the end, they walked away with a newfound sense of confidence in their ability to perform, and they became better performers on the court as a result.

Since we committed to the notion that performing was a skill, we have continued to find ways to teach our players how to perform, including drawing on the expertise of mental performance consultants and counsellors. We also used another creative approach that we learned from a session with the university's School of Dramatic Art. They taught us how the basic rules of improvisation can improve our on-court performance. The first rule of improv stipulates that someone cannot respond "no" to their acting partner's lead-in. (Imagine how detrimental to the flow of improv that would be.) We applied this rule as we ran our offensive systems and made sure to respond to a player's decision on the court in the same way. If a player decided to pass, the other players would accept the pass and continue to create from there. The second rule of improv stipulates that an actor must respond with "yes, and," which on the court translates to all five players taking any action necessary to get to where the ball was going in order to make something of any play thrown at them. That really helped players accept that there were no mistakes, and that a competition is in fact a creative process.

Once accountability was established, I did not have to intervene as much. Veterans now teach the rookies how we do things and what is expected of them as Lancers. During practices, if the tone or effort isn't up to par, the leaders take care of it, and it starts with using language that inspires and empowers rather than restricts. The same goes for performance; the team autocorrects and leads itself. This is really when a coach knows the culture of excellence has been established, and this helps a team move through painful periods of inevitable grind on the path to becoming champions.

CHAPTER 10

Planning for the Grind

"Keep your eyes on the sun, and you will not see the shadows."

—PROVERB

After six years of dedicated work to our vision, we were the defending national champions for the first time in our history, looking to start a new season fresh as September and the beginning of school came around. Yet our team identity felt lost. Our star players returned from a summer in Europe out of shape. Our local players were demotivated, and I, too, wasn't sure I wanted to embark on another year of so much effort and so many sacrifices. I had worked six years of my life in order to achieve one goal, and I had achieved it. So now what? The thought of returning to training camp for a new season was painful. No one wanted to be there. I asked a former colleague of mine who had won many national championships for advice. "You have a championship hangover," he said. "Players do not want to be in training camp; they just want to play and win again."

The grind is a difficult test for all athletes and coaches, and whether it is experienced after a big win or in a season that is not going as planned, it is inevitable. The grind takes hold of a team when motivation is low, purpose slips out of sight, and the vision feels out of reach. From a player's perspective, this may take the form of an unexpected setback such as dealing with nagging injuries, never-ending rehab, or simply the daily life of a student-athlete—missing classes for competition, rushing from school to practice, eating on the go, and a slim social life. The grind is not any kinder to coaches. It can be tough to stay motivated when dealing with extensive travel, internal conflicts, unfruitful recruiting, athletes and assistants who lack commitment, countless hours of administrative work, and, of course, a lack of proper support systems.

Furthermore, the job of coaching, with its demanding nature and its multitude of challenges, can not only become a grind but contribute to potential burnout. Research has found that up to 25 percent of coaches experience symptoms of burnout as each competitive season draws to an end, due to the significant pressures, extended working hours, passion for the sport, and the absence of job security. Add to that unpredictable situations that inevitably crop up. Through the years, I have found that maintaining a strong team culture through direct coaching and managing the environment have enabled me and my team to get through grind periods more efficiently.

TIME-OUT

Urban Meyer is one of only a handful of college football coaches in NCAA history who successfully built a national winning program at two different schools: the University of Florida in 2006 and 2008, and Ohio State in 2015. A key element of his success has been his blue-red-gold (BRG) incentive-based system. The BRG system contains inputs and outputs focused on improving player motivation and consists of factors such as the athlete's effort, attitude, grade point average, and off-the-field behaviours. Failure to meet the demands required in each level results in consequences such as mandatory study hall sessions and early morning gatherings to clean the weight room and player lounge. Urban Meyer's incentive-based system has proven to be effective in developing national-championship-winning teams and ensures his players are prepared to succeed off the field.[1]

COACHING THE ATHLETES: DESIGNING A YEARLY TRAINING PLAN

Every year, to ensure optimal performance and maintain high levels of motivation, I implement a comprehensive approach called the yearly training plan (YTP). This coaching plan involves thorough periodization and strategic planning, enabling athletes to stay committed throughout long grind periods, allowing us to focus on the daily tasks that may seem mundane but serve as building blocks for success. Periodization is a structured approach to planning and organizing training programs over time. It involves breaking down an athlete's training into distinct phases or periods, each with specific goals, intensities, and training focuses. The primary purpose of periodization is to optimize an athlete's performance while minimizing the risk of overtraining or injury, and I found it to be the best tool to successfully work through the grind. The key components of periodization that I work with are:

1. **Macrocycle:** This is the longest training period and typically spans a year or a competitive season. (We use one year.) The macrocycle is divided into several phases to allow for gradual progression and peak performance at specific times. Within the macrocycle, there are distinct phases, which include the following:

   - **General Preparation:** This phase focuses on building a foundation of fitness and addressing weaknesses. Athletes work on increasing their muscular strength and power. It often includes weightlifting, resistance training, plyometrics, and running to improve endurance and aerobic capacity. For basketball specifically, it involves lower-intensity, high-volume training such as open scrimmages and long periods of shooting the ball.
   - **Specific Preparation:** During this phase, athletes work on increasing their muscular power and anaerobic capacity. With basketball, it includes coach-directed individual skills training sessions and more targeted scrimmages or open gyms.
   - **Pre-competition:** This phase emphasizes explosive movements and speed. Athletes work on converting their strength into power through activities like sprinting, jumping, and agility drills. This is also when training camp and team training starts.

- **Tapering:** Tapering is a crucial aspect of periodization. It involves reducing the training load and volume in the weeks leading up to a competition. This allows athletes to recover, reduce fatigue, and perform at their best during the competitive phase. Tapering is essential to peaking, and we do it by increasing the intensity of practice while reducing the volume of all skills, training, and practices.
- **Competition or Peak Phase:** In this phase, athletes focus on sharpening their skills and maintaining their peak fitness level. The focus is all on performance.
- **Transition:** Adequate rest, nutrition, and recovery strategies are integrated into periodization plans to prevent overtraining and ensure athletes stay healthy and motivated. These happen throughout the season, and there is also a two-week complete break at the end of the season.

2. **Mesocycle:** The mesocycle is a shorter training block within the macrocycle, lasting several weeks to a few months. Each mesocycle is designed with a particular training focus, such as endurance, strength, power, or skill development.

3. **Microcycle:** The microcycle is the shortest training period, typically lasting one week. It outlines the daily training activities and includes variations in intensity, volume, and specific workouts. A microcycle can include different types of training sessions like strength training, endurance workouts, skill practice, and recovery days.

To effectively execute this approach, I created my YTP in the form of a graph and subsequently complemented it with a detailed strategic plan in written form. These plans are shared with the team annually, ensuring a comprehensive understanding of the rationale behind our training methods. Athletes know when to push their limits, when to allow for rest and recovery, and how each phase relates to their overall development. This clarity provides them with a road map for their journey, emphasizing the significance of present-day efforts in achieving future success.

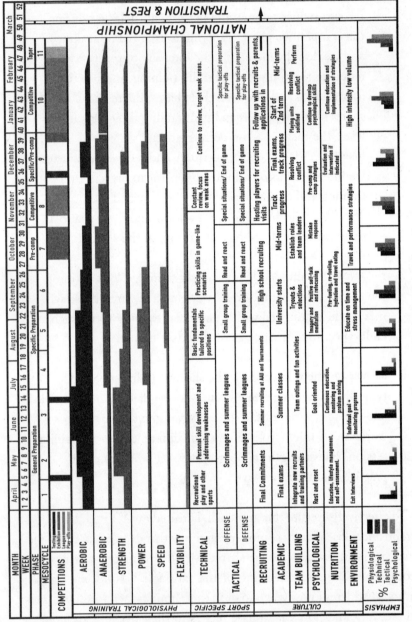

Figure 9: Yearly Training Plan and Periodization

By adhering to this plan, we can effectively train our athletes to peak at the right time and perform at their best during playoffs.

DETAILING AN INDIVIDUAL TRAINING PLAN

The YTP has proven to be a great tool to manage the grind as it points to where each player is headed and why the team is engaged in a certain type of training. It also helps coaches avoid distractions or feeling overwhelmed. It is absolutely crucial that each player understands where they fit in and how they can contribute to the team's yearly objectives; otherwise, they would inevitably lose focus, motivation, and their sense of purpose.

To ensure this does not happen, we created an additional tool: the individualized training plan (ITP). Figure 10 shows that by identifying each player's strengths and weaknesses, we can create a personalized road map that outlines the specific areas they need to work on. This personalized approach enables players to stay focused and motivated on their individual goals and helps them buy into the team's vision.

An ITP not only helps our players develop their skills but also helps me identify gaps in the team's overall performance and therefore understand our recruitment needs.

To create ITPs, I begin from the long-term vision and then break it into achievable individualized goals (IGs) for each player. This involves a serious amount of effort to execute continuous goal setting down to the smallest denominator possible for each player. I then work backwards once again from our vision and break down goals for each player to focus on. I attempt to pinpoint every goal, drill, intervention, and piece of feedback to ensure that each training exercise clearly points to the IGs. Over time, we notice a stronger commitment, increased motivation, and more hard work put forth by our athletes.

The team's vision and YTP, along with focus on players' ITPs and how each fits into the bigger picture, allow me to build a winning team culture that drives success on the court. By adhering to this plan, we avoid deflating situations that can lead to exhaustion and burnout.

I was inspired to use this technique based on the psychological research of Bandura and Schunk. These two researchers worked with two groups of

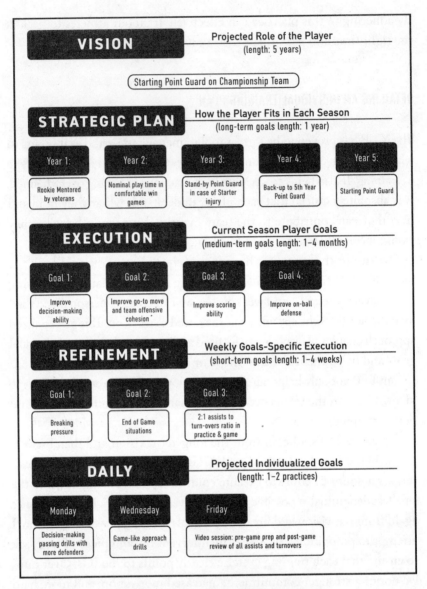

Figure 10: Five-Step Individual Training Plan

children aged seven to ten and asked them to complete 42 pages of math problems in seven sessions. Group 1 was told to set a goal of completing six pages of math problems per session. Group 2 was told to set a goal of completing all 42 pages of math problems over seven sessions as they wished. You may have guessed that group 1 was more effective at executing the task of completing all 42 pages. Setting smaller subgoals was found to be easier to achieve and brought more accurate answers than one large goal.[2]

I might not have placed such emphasis on meticulous planning for each season or on the long-term plan without my research findings. However, the results are clear and undeniable. They confirmed what many expert coaches have long asserted: building a successful program requires more than just excellent tactical knowledge (*X*s and *O*s), and it also requires more than being a very organized person. While organization and planning are important, they alone do not make someone a championship coach. The key lies in the ability to intersect all these qualities masterfully. An effective coach of a championship team combines thorough organizational skills with plans for growth of each individual while maintaining the alignment of the broader vision.

MANAGING THE ENVIRONMENT: UNFORESEEN CIRCUMSTANCES

At a leadership conference I spoke at in 2019, I asked a few hundred top business executives and HR personnel, "What comes to mind when you think of a coach?" The responses included a motivator, someone who gives direction from the sidelines, a patient teacher, a whistle and a loud voice, someone who spends hours watching game film, a leader, and so on. One gentleman described a championship celebration that showed players pouring the Gatorade jug over their coach. While these answers have a touch of reality, they relate to only one part of a coach's work: directly coaching athletes. In fact, what takes up most of our time is the planning, evaluating, and decision-making that goes on behind the scenes, not the direction and leadership itself. Coaches constantly manage the environment, facing unexpected challenges that require quick thinking and agile management.

In one instance, I had such severe food poisoning that I did not sleep all night after a six-hour bus trip to an away game. The next day, at game time, I was on the bench with a garbage pail to my right, coaching as best I could. Several times, we got caught in snowstorms, in airports overnight, on a bus for eight hours stranded, without eating, stressed out as we passed cars and semi-trucks rolled over on the highway. The never-ending begging for money (professionally called fundraising) that we must continually ask of our community. Parents yelling from the stands to put their daughters in the game or giving us the cold shoulder if we do not play their daughters. Boosters being so offended that their favourite player did not finish the game they pull their donations from the program. Referees overcontrolling the game or being offended and making unfair calls. A colleague being unreasonable. A boss not listening or being patronizing. And probably the winner of the most unexpected situation I had to deal with: we suddenly had not one but two 22-year-old players dealing with some serious heartbreak ... and they were heartbroken over the same person. I had felt that those two players were battling harder at practice, but it wasn't until later that I heard the full story. So many times I have said, "If we could just coach!" Well, the truth is all of these unforeseen circumstances are part of coaching, and I have experienced these kinds of situations in my career as a high school coach, university coach, national team coach, and professional coach. It took me a while to accept that my work extends beyond the court. The storms faced in the greater coaching context are inevitable, and it is my responsibility to prepare for them. Coaching is not only running practices, playing games, and leading. It is about taking all those realities that form the grind and finding a way to conquer them head-on, with full force. Of course, this is easier said than done. But accepting that the grind is a part of the job is a step in the right direction.

Beyond periodization, vision, direction, individual goals, and the acceptance of dealing with unforeseen circumstances, there was a particular situation that led me to finally create a framework to help me deal with the grind. We were about to board our plane for our fifth national championship bid when we received a devastating blow. A rival school had filed a complaint against us, accusing one of our players of intentionally injuring one of their players during the qualifying playoff game. The opposing school was requesting our removal from the Elite Eight national tournament. It was chaos. Endless phone calls and emails flew back and forth between myself, the athletic director, and the league with video reviews and investigations thrown into the mix. The stress and distraction were almost unbearable. I had to find a way to block out this new reality and manage as best I could. When I thought things couldn't get any worse, I was informed that our entire coaching staff was being investigated for allegedly suggesting that our player injure the opposing athlete on purpose. This was absolutely false. It took an immense amount of mental strength and focus to push through this nightmare and work at preparing the team for the national championship quarter-finals game ahead.

During the tournament, I sat down and sketched Figure 11 in my journal. It depicted how I could differentiate managing my coaching environment from directly coaching the athletes. This image has since become a powerful tool for me to stay focused on the task at hand and block out distraction, no matter how chaotic any situation may get. It is also made it clear to me that leading—or direct coaching—and managing are two different skills set that must be mastered. Thankfully, the complaint was eventually shown to be baseless, and the investigation was closed a few days after we had won our fifth national championship.

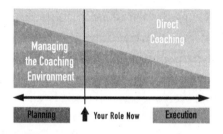

 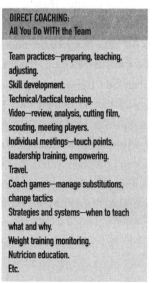

Figure 11: The Manager-Coach Continuum

Figure 11 is a valuable tool for coaches facing challenges beyond direct coaching. It helps maintain focus on the primary task of coaching while also managing the environment in which the team operates. Skilled coaches adeptly navigate between these roles and teach their team leaders to do the same. Being aware of our position on this spectrum at any given moment helps ensure that the demands of management do not overshadow our primary task of direct coaching. Without this awareness, management challenges can consume all our thoughts and time, ultimately undermining our leadership capacities and well-being.

This concept applies to leaders in all fields. Effective leaders are those who can set direction, reflect, make informed decisions, and drive progress. However, challenges arise when managing difficult people or circumstances. The grind is an inevitable part of any leader's journey, whether dealing with losses, illnesses, demanding personalities, administrative red tape, financial cuts, or any unexpected situation. Leaders must find balance on this continuum and not get dragged down by the overwhelming demands that managing the environment imposes.

It is crucial to remember that there's a plan in place and a road map to follow to ensure that everyone stays on track. Even during the most challenging periods, leaders must remain creative and find a way to overcome obstacles and advance their teams. It's not just about skill and strategy; it's also about grit and perseverance. By maintaining a clear perspective and a focus on the end goal, leaders and teams can rise above even the most difficult circumstances, as they ascend to their championship successfully.

Stories like these are a part of my coaching life that most people do not think about. When coaches are forced to step out of directly coaching athletes, that, in and of itself, is a real grind to deal with. Each year, I find myself wondering if another coach has it better at another institution, but I am quickly reminded that while limitations and circumstances may be different elsewhere, they always arise. So, we commit to crushing our own contextual roadblocks, no matter what they are.

CHAPTER 11

The Glue That Holds It Together

"The bond that links your true family is not one of blood, but of respect and joy in each other's life."

—RICHARD BACH

I had the incredible opportunity to spend two days with renowned All Blacks coach Wayne Smith at his home in Cambridge, New Zealand, and witness their culture firsthand. During our time together, I asked Coach Smith what accomplishment made him the most proud. His face lit up as he shared his personalized All Blacks book—a special memento, bestowed upon notable players upon their retirement, or in Coach Smith's case, when he transitioned from player to coach. The book was a heartfelt compilation of quotes, pictures, and messages from his teammates, serving as a cherished reminder of the bonds they had formed. With genuine emotion, Coach Smith turned the pages, expressing, "These men are the reason I am who I am today." He never mentioned winning.

For Coach Smith, the memories and connections with his teammates were far more valuable than any accolades or championship titles. This reinforced for me the notion that the ultimate triumph lies in the journey itself, in the collective growth, unity, and enduring bonds forged along the way. The All Blacks create a learning environment based on strong, trusting relationships with each other, in turn creating space for them to show their vulnerability. They work on their own mental and emotional weaknesses through various means, including sessions with psychologists. Personal growth exercises lead to newfound coping skills that lay the foundation to outperform their competitors under pressure. Of course, their organization is filled with the most skilled rugby players and coaches who have a desire to win. However, personal growth is the non-negotiable and winning the by-product—not the other way around.

High-level athletics is a grind with constant demands. During this entire quarter, we've been looking at strategies that help us rise above the grind: vision and detailed planning, setting goals for athletes, and creating a strong team culture. The final piece of the puzzle—the one that glues it all together—comes back to me, the coach. As a leader, I have to make difficult and unpopular, yet necessary, decisions while maintaining positive personal relationships with players and keeping the team cohesive. Failing to do this can quickly plunge the team into a downward spiral and certainly will not build the trust necessary to pull everyone through the grind.

When I have to make a hard decision, I remember Walt Disney's words: "When your values are clear to you, making decisions becomes easier." Back in 2013, our Windsor Lancers basketball program had already won three national championships, and the majority of our players were returning. During the pre-season, we received an invitation to play a couple of exhibition games against the senior women's national team from Argentina. We were thrilled to be invited and began preparing for the games by setting up an early training camp in August. This was when things got interesting.

As the last training camp practice ended, I received a strange phone call from a concerned friend. The informant reported that some players had broken serious team values. I told my two captains about the call. They asked me how I wanted to deal with it. I told them to bring the culprits to my office, and I went in to wait for them.

While I was waiting, I decided that whoever had behaved badly (probably a couple of rookies, I thought) would not be going on the upcoming trip. It was a decision based on the team's values and accountability. I heard voices in the hallway, and in came five players. It was almost half of the team, including three of my star players! I had to make a tough decision. I told them they were not coming and that I would contact them upon our return about what would happen next. The team flew out the next day with only seven players. With no one to bring the ball up the floor, we lost by 50 points. Five. Zero. I apologized to the head coach of Team Argentina who, of course, was expecting to play a much better Lancer team. It was a painful trip for the program.

When we returned, the five players met with me, apologized, and worked harder than ever for the team. The sense of respect was high. The team went undefeated that season and won their fourth consecutive national championship. The obstacle of the off-season had made us grow in purposeful ways. Not making that decision would have allowed a laissez-faire culture to creep in and increase confusion. It would have threatened our trust, cohesiveness, and meaningful relationships. Hard decisions always advance the greater good of the team in the long run.

It is essential to have built strong and positive personal relationships with the players that allow for trust and collaboration to continue once the hard decision is made. Gilbert Enoka, the mental performance consultant of the All Blacks, drove this home to me: "Relationships above results" and "Relationships trump everything." When you invest in your relationships with coaches, teammates, and support staff, you create a support system that can carry you through the toughest of times on and off the court. By focusing on relationships, the All Blacks have built a culture of trust, respect, and loyalty. They understand that their success is not just about their individual talents but about the collective effort of the entire organization.

TIME-OUT

A 2020 study investigated how high-performance coaches managed difficult athletes. The results indicated that these coaches identified problem athletes early, established meaningful relationships with them, and transformed their behaviours to match the team culture (although this was not always possible). Coaches spoke about the importance of empowering their athlete leaders with the responsibility of instilling the coach's values and vision with difficult athletes.[1] In management, exploring ways to empower employees and leaders to handle difficult colleagues would be worth exploring.

At Windsor, we, too, believe in the power of meaningful relationships. When we do not have good team cohesion, our accountability wavers, and our performance suffers. When we stay together, we grow together, and that is when the magic happens. Our approach is centred on creating a family atmosphere: we promote acceptance of each other as we are. It's a model that has worked well for our context, which is made up of student-athletes who are teenagers to young adults. Here are the five key principles we use for our basketball family.

1. Set Boundaries

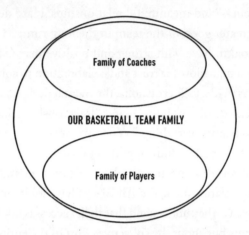

I like to draw an image of a basketball family that is made up of two sub-teams: the coaches and the players. The coaches' team is "all one," with one voice and one direction set by the head coach. This means we don't have good cop, bad cop scenarios. Instead, when the coaches are unhappy about a performance, all coaches are unhappy. Our most successful teams have been those where players knew that if one coach said no, every coach would stand by the same decision. This pushes the players to rally behind the decision, as opposed to dividing the team and breeding mistrust. The players are quick to notice the coaching team bond, and they are always drawn to do the same.

I found this to work so much better than to divide the coaching staff into opposite roles and leadership styles. This disconnection can create an environment where players and coaches create unhealthy bonds with each other because they are kinder or nicer than the head coach, or vice versa. A good cop, bad cop model is likely to create division within the team and propel the "family" into a dysfunctional operating unit as shown below:

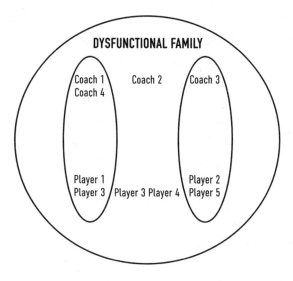

We also add an outer circle linked to, but not a part of, our specific basketball family. This is our extended family, which includes our fans, parents, sponsors, significant others, the school's athletic department, and anyone else remotely connected to us in one way or another throughout the season. This diagram is helpful for team members to understand that if parents or fans are not happy with players' performances or coaches' decisions on playing time, their input cannot affect our immediate basketball family dynamic.

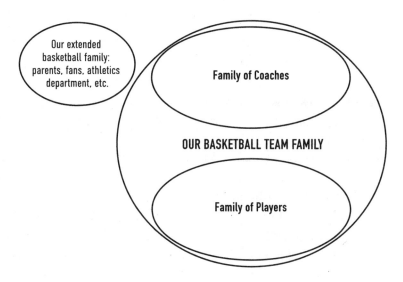

Players are encouraged to prioritize our team's way of thinking over what they hear from someone in the extended family who doesn't understand all variables for decision-making. This prompts players to check in with us, instead of them, asking for clarification if something doesn't seem right or if they are frustrated. We teach that a healthy and loving family is a place where members hold each other accountable.

Just like a real family, not every situation is a walk in the park. In my early years, I was less open to players' needs and opinions and was often a poor communicator. Our coaching staff was not always united, and some players never got to trust us enough as coaches and eventually left the team. Once we found a good core group of coaches and players, we found that the family structure we created worked wonders for the health of the entire organization, strengthened our team culture, and helped us through the grind. We operated on the same page with a sense of togetherness, we pushed in the same direction, we managed conflict resolution quickly, and we genuinely learned to love each other as family members. We won championships, but the focus was on trusting our relationships. As a result, the team reached a great operating space, even in the wake of difficult situations and decisions.

TIME-OUT
Research shows that high-quality coaching consists of an ability to foster a nurturing climate that creates strong interpersonal relationships. One strategy for showing support and building quality coach-athlete relationships is tactile communication, which includes non-verbal actions such as high-fives, handshakes, and fist bumping during practices and games.[2]

2. **Choose Truth over Harmony**
During a coaching seminar with the Canadian national team program, I learned about the principle of truth versus harmony, which I quickly adopted as a tangible action. Successful leaders

cannot always act in a way that upholds harmony between them and a team member, and it is a misconception to think that team success comes from trying to keep everyone happy. Even if the truth hurts, it is a key to success. What's worse is when members of a team feel they have been misled by the leader; the failure to be clear and tell the truth, for fear of offending, becomes the cause of team dysfunction.

This concept resonated with me because in the past my inexperience led me to spend most of the year trying to keep my team happy and harmonious, instead of being truthful about playing time for players. My communication was not always clear, and some players became frustrated. Being made aware of this forced me to adjust and improve—but it took courage. How do we tell someone there is a better player or that their performance is not up to par? How do we ask a player not to take a shot when we allow that very same shot to be taken by another player? The key is to remember that speaking the truth is not an excuse to berate. The leader must deliver feedback in a careful, non-threatening way, filled with compassion. Certainly, when presented with truthful expectations and transparency, some team members feel upset, but it allows for clarity and peace. It shifts the onus onto the player. It forces them to grieve and move forward or simply move on, allowing us to press onward towards the team's vision.

A coach who has mastered this principle is Gregg Popovich, long-time head coach of the NBA's San Antonio Spurs. Pop tells it like it is, often leaving his players on edge, yet there is profound respect and love in their relationships. The trust established between him and his players allows them to accept his brutally honest feedback on performance. Pop's relationship with superstar centre Tim Duncan is a great example. Pop did not spare his words and offered more than his fair share of bluntness about Duncan's performance. In spite of this, on the night of Duncan's retirement, he said, through tears, "Thank you, Coach Pop, for being more than a coach to me, for being like a father to me, thank you." In the end, telling the truth takes courage—and a lot of practice. I can attest that my players responded to this approach with so much more respect and commitment to our team and culture, even the bench players who saw little or no playing time.

3. Listen to Players' Voices

During the qualifying playoff game for the 2014 national tournament, our team was down by double digits in the fourth quarter. We were trying to figure out how to turn the game around. And then in a time-out, from out of nowhere came Anna Mullins—a player who rarely stepped on the court— interrupting our high-level coaching discussion. She found the inner strength to interject and got our attention. We knew her basketball IQ was off the charts, but we never expected her to step up like this. She suggested a defensive adjustment that none of us had considered. And it's exactly what we needed to turn the game around. We made the change, and we turned around the double-digit deficit in less than eight minutes. The best part is that Anna's suggestion was part of her individualized goal (IG) that she had personally been practising. Not only did we win that game, later that month we won our fourth national championship. You better believe we gave Anna a shout-out in front of everyone for her clutch contribution to the victory. Moral of the story? Listen to your players! They have insight from a different angle that coaches may not see.

As coaches, we may have years of experience and extensive knowledge of the game, but it is the players who are on the court, experiencing the ebb and flow of the game in real time. By creating an environment where players feel heard and valued, we not only empower them to contribute their unique perspectives and insights but also demonstrate that we trust and respect their abilities. Anna's ability to identify a critical issue and propose a successful solution highlights the value of empowering our players to think critically and creatively, and to speak up when it counts.

4. Develop Strong Relationships

In 2020 and 2021, I had a unique opportunity to learn more about team building relationships. I assisted head coach Ryan Schmidt in the Canadian Elite Basketball League, a men's professional league. As I worked alongside Ryan, I quickly realized that his coaching style was based on two core beliefs: treating people well and building relationships. Ryan's emphasis on building relationships with the players was evident in everything he did. He had the entire coaching staff research the players' backgrounds and report their findings to the rest of the coaches. At training camp, each player was given the opportunity to present a PowerPoint about themselves, allowing everyone to get to know each other on a deeper level. Ryan consistently encouraged us to meet with players individually and spend time working out with them in the gym. It was clear that this focus on building relationships was an essential pillar of the culture he wanted to establish. As a result of Ryan's leadership, the team was highly cohesive, respectful, and accountable. Players loved playing for him and for each other, resulting in a highly successful season both on and off the court. I had witnessed a masterclass in building relationships into team culture.

I wish I had learned from Ryan earlier in my career. It would have helped me understand how to better coach one of my star players. For most of Miah-Marie Langlois's time on the Lancer team, it was like trying to mix oil and water. We just didn't see eye to eye on anything. As she was my starting point guard, it was essential to find a way to work together. So, I went to work on improving my communication and leadership skills, seeking advice from mentors and attending seminars. I tried including her in team decisions, but we kept butting heads. I never gave up on trying to get through to her and kept looking for ways to connect. Then in her last year of eligibility, we were in the playoffs, but the team was flat and needed a boost. During a critical practice, Miah-Marie pulled me aside and said, "Coach, I don't want the players to know this, but we need you to kick our butt right now. This is my last year, and I want to win.

Whatever you decide to put us through, even if it seems crazy, I'll have your back 100 percent. I'll rally the girls, and I'll make sure everyone buys in." I couldn't believe it. It was like the stars had aligned. Thanks in big part to Miah-Marie's leadership, we won another national championship.

That was definitely a turning point our relationship. After graduation, Miah-Marie went on to play for the Canadian national team, became an Olympian, and has had a long-lasting professional career and always kept in touch. Whenever she comes to visit Windsor, I feel privileged that she texts to grab breakfast and catch up. Now, several years after having coached her, we reminisce and laugh about how much our coach-player relationship was filled with hardships and headaches. She said, "I bet out of all the players you have coached, you would have never thought that we would end up friends." I agreed. I never thought I would develop a lasting friendship with Miah-Marie. Like many others on teams I have coached, she has helped recruit new players, returned to the Windsor campus to run camps, spoken many times to the team, and practised with us. She's a role model and mentor to many of our players. Witnessing this is by far the most fulfilling part of being a coach.

5. Add Joy

While I was writing this book, the COVID-19 pandemic hit, our 2020–21 season was cancelled, and some major team reflection occurred. One of the things that I personally dwelled on during the long days of lockdown was how much fun we'd had with the teams that had won past championships. While this was not a value that our team had identified in our Lancer Way documents, I felt it had been a staple of all of our national champion teams and that it was necessary to include it in light of the difficulties of the pandemic. After discussion with our team leaders, they decided unanimously to add a fifth value to the Lancer Way.

The game exists to enhance our lives.
Competing leads to highs and lows but we choose to compete for the joy it brings. Basketball does not consume us, rather it enriches us. It offers a safe place to be our best selves. It teaches us to come together in a common interest and that life is meant to be experienced to the fullest. In all forms of what competing brings us: we include laughter, happiness and joy.

Figure 12: Add Joy to the Lancer Way

I have so many memories of the joy that our basketball family has experienced over the years. A day before our 2013 season opener, Miah-Marie showed up to practice in an orthopedic walking boot and told us that she had partially torn her Achilles tendon stepping off the sidewalk on the way to school that morning. I was devastated. All the players had surrounded her and were as upset as I was. When I rallied the strength to face the situation and address the team, everyone started laughing as Miah-Marie suddenly took off the boot and went for a run. Joy allows for humour and brings in an element of lightness and playfulness that strengthens the bonds between those seeking to achieve greatness. Like author Laurence Gonzales says, being light and playful is a way to survive. Even a simple game of tag to start practice can go a long way.

During that same year, Jessica Gordon, our backup centre, knew that her court time might be limited as she was playing second to the Canadian Player of the Year. During the playoff run of our three-peat, we decided to put her in charge of making the team laugh before each game. Her creativity in finding new ways to crack us up was hilarious. For example, she once told our smallest player to hide in the team uniform bag, and when I was desperate to know where Caitlyn Longmuir was during our pre-game prep, she jumped out of the bag that had been at our feet the whole time. The effect of adding joy and laughter to our team brought our family closer, lightened the mood, and helped us perform better.

That is how you survive the grind. Instead of having a group of players show up to practice day after day and go through the motions, disinterested and unaffected, you build a family united by a common goal, give them individualized goals, and add humour. The process was more important than winning every year, and we meticulously created a plan down to the smallest detail to activate our daily actions and training goals. When our team aligned its behaviours with our values, our culture strengthened and produced results. It also created an experience everyone wanted to be a part of. Excellence, growth, strength, family, and joy are the pillars of our team culture. It's the Lancer Way. Like coach Phil Jackson said, "In basketball, like in life, true joy comes from being fully present in each and every moment, not just when things are going your way." The grind may feel inevitable, but it doesn't have to define us. When we rise above as a team and conquer the grind, the opportunities for success are endless.

QUARTER BREAK

Four Keys to Conquering the Grind

1. **BUILD A TEAM COVENANT.** Start with the end in mind. Envision and define the culture you want to create. Set clear values. Work with your team to establish performance standards that inspire everyone to excel. Be open to revising as the team develops. Have the courage to make difficult decisions based on the values established. This approach builds trust, respect, and a team poised to conquer.

2. **CREATE A YEARLY TRAINING PLAN.** Take the vision and break it into yearly themes; then divide them into smaller cycles with achievable monthly, weekly, and daily goals. From there, set individualized goals for each player. This ensures a personal sense of mission that carries players through rough patches of the long season.

3. **CONTROL WHAT YOU CAN; MANAGE WHAT YOU CAN'T.** Don't be discouraged by external factors beyond your control. Manage these circumstances as best as you can and ensure they don't detract from your leadership tasks or direct coaching efforts.

4. **BECOME A FAMILY.** Relationships before championships. Relationships trump everything.

Coach Insight: When your personal values and work values don't align, it can lead to conflict and stress. Seek out organizations that share your personal values to ensure a harmonious and fulfilling work experience.

LOOK AHEAD TO THE FOURTH QUARTER

Even with all the right elements in place, a championship isn't guaranteed. So, how can you ensure success? Keep reading to learn how to develop the necessary grit in your team and to master the journey of leading your team to the peak.

FOURTH QUARTER

The Kill

"For the strength of the pack is the wolf, and the strength of the wolf is the pack."

—RUDYARD KIPLING

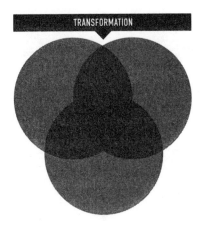

"The fourth quarter is kill" is one of the powerful sayings posted in bold in our team room. When the last quarter of the game comes around, the saying reminds us that it is time to give it all we have, time to take it home, and time to plow through the opponent. No excuses tolerated. We put all of our focus on finishing the task, leaving no space for doubt, and securing the win. The goal of coming together as a team culminates in this moment: to succeed at getting the kill. We have a "no second chances" mindset.

This is it! It's time to reap all four higher-order categories of our research model and reach transformation. The vision is established at the centre, the planning has taken place, the players have grown individually, and the coaches have become better people and leaders. All that work can now transform into success—if you learn to master it.

CHAPTER 12

Gritty Teams Win

Grit, synonymous with resiliency, embodies unwavering character, cou-
rageous spirit, and determination. It is a key factor of success not only
in sports but also in other fields, including the military. Prospective cadets
wishing to enroll at West Point (U.S. Military Academy) need to be
above-average high school students and undergo thorough physical and
mental testing. Once the cadets are accepted, they subject themselves to
an intense schedule, including a gruelling six-week "beast barracks" basic
training camp. By the end of summer, 3 percent of the cadets will have quit.
By the end of their four years of schooling, this number will have risen
to 19 percent. But why is that the case?

Angela Duckworth, a professor at the University of Pennsylvania,
researched the concept of grit and explored the reasons why 81 percent of
cadets persevered in the program at West Point. Over a span of ten years,
she focused on more than 11,000 cadets and discovered that possessing and
demonstrating grit was the most significant factor contributing to their
graduating rate. Grit even surpassed intellectual capabilities and physical
strength as an indicator of achievement. In another study conducted by
Duckworth, she aimed to identify the key factor that distinguished successful individuals in various domains, such as the military cadets, Ivy League
graduates, and National Spelling Bee finalists. The results revealed that
those with the strongest "fighting spirits" were the ones who ultimately
achieved their goals. Resilience plays a critical role in pursuing long-term

objectives. In essence, grit represents the mental power and courage that propels individuals forward when faced with adversity.

ONE GRITTY TEAM

Mental strength and grit can be developed like any other skill. I know my team has moved into this mindset and is ready when players are no longer afraid of losing, and they desire the kill. Let's revisit the eve of our chance to punch a ticket to participate in the Elite Eight and continue to defend our first national championship title. It was the playoffs, and as the number one ranked team in the country, and defending national champions, we felt confident. We were getting ready to play the University of Ottawa, a team we had lost to by over 20 points in early November. We had devised a new game plan to contain their post play, and I felt like the early loss to Ottawa was an anomaly—it was our first encounter, early in the season, and we were still suffering from our "championship hangover." Taking all this into consideration, I was convinced we would win and qualify for the Elite Eight. Yet one of our best players was struggling with some personal issues that raised concerns among her teammates. To compound matters, a stalker had infiltrated our hotel, leading us to involve the local authorities. Noticing my worry, a few of my players reassured me that they had everything under control.

When the game began, our team struggled to find a rhythm, conceding a daunting 10–0 lead within the first two minutes of play. In an attempt to regroup, we called an early time-out to regain our composure, but we only saw the lead get deeper. By halftime, coming back from the 25-point disadvantage seemed impossible. Ottawa had been playing with such fervour and had been perfect in nearly every decision. Despite our efforts to fight back, they played the best basketball game I have seen to this day in our league. Regrettably, I cannot recount a miraculous turn of events or a historic comeback. As the final seconds ticked away, I glanced at the scoreboard: our devastating defeat was by a staggering 49 points. Forty-nine. They had utterly destroyed us, left us humiliated, and, in the players' minds, taken away our dreams of qualifying to defend our national championship.

As a coaching staff, however, we knew that our season was not yet over. That year marked a trial period for an extended national championship format: introducing wild cards to be determined at a play-in tournament. Instead of being eliminated, we were now headed on this detour. As fate would have it, we were told right after the game that we had been slotted to replay the University of Ottawa in Ottawa, as part of our play-in tournament six days later. It could not have been a more difficult route to take. The team room was silent as we gathered after the game. I could not find words. We told the team to get back to the hotel, and a later meeting time would be set.

That night at the hotel, we were hard on the players. First I spoke, and then my two assistants. Even our analytics coach, Lucas, had a lot to say. We addressed the profound letdown of not showing up for a game of such significance. We wanted their attention, and we had it. Every gaze was fixed upon us, and we observed nods of acknowledgement around the room. The stark reality was that our three best guards had only managed to convert one out of 33 shots during the entire game—a disheartening statistic. We were significantly out-rebounded, and there were moments when we appeared absent on the court. There was no sense of togetherness or ownership. There was no sense of urgency, no physicality, no determination, and certainly no desire or grit. While Ottawa was an exceptional team, we were, too, and yet we suffered a 49-point defeat.

Shortly after midnight, we let the players return to their rooms and told them the bus was departing at six the next morning. We were exhausted, and we had to get back on the bus to drive nine hours from Ottawa to Windsor. In exactly three days, we would have to hop on that same bus to return for another nine-hour trip back to Ottawa to claim the wild card. There was no room for rest or self-pity.

That night, a fire alarm went off at the hotel, startling us awake around 2 a.m. The sound of people yelling "Fire!" filled the hallways, and we could hear the sirens approaching, leaving us with no choice but to quickly descend 23 flights of stairs. We gathered nervously in the stairwell and hurried down until we reached the ground-level door, which opened directly onto the cold, snowy sidewalk. The temperature was a bone-chilling −22 degrees Celsius, and we found ourselves standing there in our pyjamas for over 30 minutes, waiting to be allowed back inside. It was a harsh experience.

After some time, the firefighters told us it was safe to return to our rooms, but we still couldn't use the elevators. Wanting nothing more than to get some rest, I signalled to the team to start climbing the stairs again. My calf muscles ached for days afterward, and I can only imagine how exhausted my players felt.

The following morning on the bus, everyone appeared worn out. Personally, I hadn't managed to sleep at all, and I felt physically ill. Even my assistant coach Tom looked pale and drained. Ottawa had not only left us battered physically, but our egos were also deeply bruised. The long journey and the hotel ordeal had only added to the overwhelming sense of mental and physical exhaustion. I was certain the players felt the same way. The bus ride was eerily quiet, with not a single word uttered, not even during our meal stop. Throughout the entire nine-hour journey, I racked my brain, desperately searching for a solution for our team.

During my contemplation, I received a call from a close friend who was a huge fan of the team. She had taken it upon herself to purchase plastic bracelets with a shocking yet motivational message engraved on them. It was brilliant. The sight of those simple bracelets sparked my creativity. By the next morning, I had a plan in place. I sent a text to the team captains: "Come prepared to venture outdoors after practice tonight. Bring warm clothing suitable for running."

LAY YOUR BURDENS AT THE FOOT OF THE HILL

That day was supposed to be a day off, and I was well aware of how exhausted we all were. However, that was precisely the point I wanted to emphasize. I wanted them to realize that they had more energy and determination than they believed. Stepping into the meeting room, I projected an air of dissatisfaction, intentionally keeping them on edge. I began by telling them that we needed to rally around a new shared vision with a shorter-term focus, and I handed out the bracelets, one by one. "These two words will be our purpose from now on, and we will respond accordingly," I declared. (We made a pact as a team to never disclose the specific words engraved on the bracelets.) I noticed a smile on the faces of one of my captains. I knew she liked it, and it gave me confidence to continue. I instructed them to wrap the bracelets around their arms and secure them with athletic tape for practice. They were not allowed to remove them until we triumphed over Ottawa. On our way to the gym for practice, we instructed the players to each pick up a 20-pound weight from the weight room. We dedicated our practice solely to toughness both strategically and physically in rebounding, offensive cuts, and mental resilience.

When practice concluded, I directed them to meet at a nearby park that boasted a large hill. The players followed my instructions. As we arrived at the base of the hill, each player clutched her weight. As they stood at the bottom of the hill, with their weights in hand, I reminded them of our mission to conquer the mountain we had set for ourselves that season.

As mentioned earlier, each quest for a national championship used a metaphor of summiting a mountain. This year, our mission was to conquer K2, known as the Savage Mountain, a nickname earned due to its treacherous nature that has claimed the lives of climbers who don't approach it with the utmost attention and focus. While its peak stands slightly lower than Everest, it is steeper, more demanding, and deadlier, with a staggering 20 percent fatality rate among climbers. Now, as the players looked at the hill, I wanted them to visualize themselves at the base of K2, gazing up at the summit and the challenging path that lay ahead. How could we move forward and bring about the necessary change to ensure that the mountain wouldn't deny us again in Ottawa? Pacing back and forth before my team, I delivered a motivational speech. "We are seasoned climbers, and by some stroke of luck in the tournament format, we have been granted a second chance to climb. But this time, it will be more challenging. We opted for a longer, more arduous and difficult route. Are you willing to seize the moment and earn the right to continue our ascent this time? Two days ago, you faltered. This time, failure will mean the death of the team and put an end to our season. Are you the defending national champions? Will you rise to the occasion?"

The players stared at me fearlessly, unwavering in their determination. One of our mentally toughest players locked eyes with me, almost defiantly, and asked, "How many times, Coach?" as she pointed at the hill currently in front of us. She was inquiring about the number of times I would request they run up and down the hill. I paused, meeting her gaze directly. "Forty-nine," I replied. Not a single player reacted or made a sound. They began to rally each other. After only a few steps, I stopped them. "Wait . . . why are you still carrying those 20-pound weights? I never asked you to. I never said you had to. All I said was 'pick up a weight on your way to practice.' It was your choice to carry it into the gym and to the park and now up this hill. Can you see how this is like the real burden and weight you've been carrying all along on your own shoulders? It's time to let go. Release your burdens, your pressures, your worries, and your fears. Climb free from the weight. Ascend without worries or fear. Rely on your own abilities, your experience. Believe in who you are and what you've already accomplished. You've all climbed successfully before. You know the way and how to reach the top. Support one another. Let go of this weight, physically and emotionally, and begin the climb." The players dropped their weights. It was as if they were undergoing a mental and perhaps even spiritual purification, releasing their fears.

Once ready, they interlocked their arms and began slowly climbing the hill. At that point, I had already made it up the hill, and from my vantage point at the summit, I could see them approaching. Something extraordinary was unfolding before my eyes—the team, with their sights set firmly on the summit, advanced steadily and confidently. As they drew closer, my assistants and I started shouting, "You're almost there! Stay focused on the peak! Stay focused on the goal!" When they reached the summit, they erupted in jubilation and celebration, and they joined in with screams of relief and joy. The energy in the air was electric! Their voices reverberated with intensity. I will forever cherish the image of a player, tears streaming down her face, exclaiming, "I AM FREE!" The message was understood. There was no need (nor intention) to have them do this 48 more times.

A gentle snowfall had begun to fall, adding an extra layer of beauty to the experience of reaching the summit—screams, embraces, and tears. I said, "You see, you can reach the summit. All you need to do is repeat the same process this Friday. The game is in your mind." Ultimately, they climbed the hill only once, unhurriedly, unburdened. And that was enough. Everyone took a deep breath, and the team gathered in a huddle. They engaged in a collective conversation, although we couldn't discern their words. When they broke the huddle, they chanted, "K2!" They were now prepared to conquer the summit. I said, "See you on the bus Wednesday." We did not meet or practice again until game day.

I do not know what the players did on Tuesday, but I slept for a long time. The Wednesday bus ride to Ottawa was as quiet as the return to Windsor had been. Except this time, it was a quiet confidence.

On the night of our game against Ottawa, my assistants and I made a deliberate choice to forgo our usual attire of suits and meticulously styled hair. Instead, we showed up in matching Lancer navy-blue team polo shirts, paired with khaki pants, and my trademark coaching ponytail. As we entered the team room, the girls, accustomed to seeing us in suits, were surprised. "We intentionally decided not to dress up tonight," I explained, "because, in all honesty, we weren't supposed to be playing. By wearing our coaches' practice gear, every time you look at us, we want you to be reminded that this game requires something *extra*. Extra work. Extra effort. Extra determination. Extra strength to secure the ball and fight for rebounds. Extra focus in your shot selection. Extra effort to make precise passes. Extra determination to extend yourself and catch those passes." I pointed to our blue attire. "We wear blue because it is more than just a colour. It symbolizes our team, our unity, our commitment. We bleed blue together. Tonight, you will work tirelessly until the job is done. Now, go out there, play your hearts out, and continue the climb just as you know how. We are ready."

It was a hard-fought game. Ottawa was still peaking and playing their best basketball, so we battled for every single possession. As the game went on, we were not able to push past them by a lot. We hung on to a slim two- to three-point advantage most of the game. There was blood, sweat, and tears. The game had the calibre of a national championship final. In the fourth quarter, one of our veterans challenged the rest of the team: "It's time to kill." I felt a strong spirit of resiliency move through our team. We fought our best and ended up winning by three points. After losing to this team by 20 points in November and 49 points six days prior, we finally had done it!

I was genuinely impressed by our team's display of grit and physicality. Despite the challenging and exhausting week we had endured, we were filled with an indescribable surge of energy. We knew that our hard-fought victory meant we had secured a spot in the 2012 Elite Eight national championship, even though it was through a wild card entry. The manner of our qualification didn't matter anymore; what mattered was that we were in. We now had the opportunity to defend our national title. As we gathered in the team room, our eyes turned to the poster we had carried throughout our journey, depicting the path to the summit of K2. In line with our revised plan, we had finally reached camp three after enduring a perilous detour. Without wasting any time, we shifted our focus to the upcoming national championship. The next challenge was the most crucial one. This mountain had taught us that talent alone doesn't guarantee victory; grit does.

TIME-OUT

Resilience is a dynamic process widely regarded as crucial to mental toughness. It involves navigating challenges, adversities, and stressors. Research indicates that building resilience is key to maintaining both well-being and performance. This is accomplished through an individual's personal qualities and their ability to positively evaluate and respond to stressors and adversity.[1]

2012 NATIONAL CHAMPIONSHIP

Feeling mentally stronger and fuelled by the messages on our bracelets, we arrived in Calgary ready to battle for the 2012 Elite Eight national championship. Our team had fallen to fourth place, and we were set to face Acadia University, a conference champion ranked fifth, in the first round. Their key player, a six-foot-tall guard with an impressive 45 percent three-point shooting average, was our primary focus. We assigned Bojana Kovacevic, our best defender, to guard her, and we knew that stopping her would mean stopping their team. Little did we expect that Bojana would not even let the Acadian guard take a decent three-point shot attempt. We dominated the game, winning by an impressive 30-point margin.

Next, in the Final Four, we had to unite to battle against the University of Calgary, the host team. The sold-out crowd offered a hostile atmosphere. In one of the loudest and most challenging environments we had ever played, we emerged victorious over Calgary, securing our spot in the championship game.

Here we were: headed to the championship final. This was our third game in three days, and in a determined affair, we beat the University of British Columbia with so much inner strength and confidence that nothing could stop us. There was no other way to describe what we accomplished but incredible. It was a formidable turnaround for a team that had nearly been eliminated. Our grit was beyond what I had seen in our team in our first national championship run. The players had tapped into something deep down inside themselves. After the game, opposing head coach Deb Huband, a seasoned veteran with more than two decades of coaching experience under her belt and three national championship wins, said we were the most physical team she had ever played against.

I had not expected to win back-to-back national championships, especially after the debacle in Ottawa. Once the on-court celebrations were done, my assistants and I entered the team room. We expected the players to be going wild, but instead we were met with total silence. The team was huddled in the middle of the room. After a few long seconds, the team exploded in cheers and revealed the Bronze Baby national championship trophy, with each of their bracelets hanging around her neck. It is a memory I will never forget. The resolute two-word message on these bracelets led us much further than a repeat. It led us to ultimately win five in a row. Yes, the teams we coached were talented, but even with our talents we had been defeated at times. We attribute our victories much more to our fitness, mental strength, and resilience. Gritty teams win.

CHAPTER 13

Grit-Boosting Techniques

Winning consecutive championships has profoundly reshaped my understanding of grit. Throughout my coaching career, I have been known for my demanding nature and high expectations of toughness. However, it was the devastating loss to Ottawa, the transformative night on the hill, and our remarkable ability to shift our mindset that prompted me to re-evaluate my approach. I realized that merely demanding mental toughness from my players was not enough; it was my duty to actively teach them how to develop it.

Over the years, I have refined a repertoire of techniques aimed at fostering grit in our players inclusive of self-confidence, emotional intelligence, and leadership maturity. These practices have proven effective in nurturing these essential qualities that lay the foundation for our success on and off the court. Here are my five best tried and true practices that yield remarkable results in developing grit.

1. **Physical Strength Equals Mental Strength**

   During my time as an assistant coach on Canada's national team program over many summers, I had the opportunity to attend a presentation from exercise physiologist Ed McNeely. One of his slides featured a simple yet powerful formula: physical strength equals mental strength. This equation conveyed a clear message: the greater an individual's physical fitness and strength, the longer they can sustain effort and the less likely they are to succumb to mental fatigue or give up. In other words, a significant degree of resilience and grit can be cultivated through improving one's physical fitness. I use this equation constantly with my team, and this is why one of our team values in the Lancer Way is strength.

Returning from the national team camp, I set a strong emphasis on physical endurance by raising our fitness standards. That year, I implemented Sunday cardio after our return from weekend competitions. We would take Mondays off instead. The reasoning behind this change was rooted in the national championship structure, which consisted of an Elite Eight tournament played on three consecutive days. A national champion had to win on Friday, Saturday, and Sunday. We tried to recreate a way to mentally match the load and demand of the championship weekend. Our league games were on Fridays and Saturdays, and whether we were at home on or on the road on Sundays, we incorporated a tough spin class upon our return.

The simple act of overcoming mental hurdles, particularly after long bus trips, proved to be beneficial. It enhanced our fitness levels and also our grit. Every Sunday, we dedicated ourselves to both physical and mental exertion, envisioning ourselves winning the championship. As a result, when the tournament arrived in March, we felt prepared. Each time we competed for the national title, we approached the Sunday championship game knowing that we had been training on Sundays all year long. Although the players may not have particularly enjoyed it in the moment, their joy was immeasurable when a gold medal was placed around their necks.

TIME-OUT

Research shows that sport offers a powerful mechanism for the empowerment of women on both physical and psychological levels. It can be used as a means of not only becoming mentally resilient on the court but also resisting social stigma and stereotypes in everyday life.[1]

2. The Key to Self-Confidence . . . Is a Key!

Self-confidence is the inner belief in one's ability to succeed, and it brings a wide range of benefits that can elevate your mindset and overall success in any area of life. Elevating confidence levels in players is one of my paramount objectives. One of the most staggering discoveries of my coaching career was how little self-confidence most of my athletes have initially. You might expect champions to have all the confidence in the world, but this simply isn't the case. After working with both men and women, I can attest that struggling with self-confidence is an issue across the board and is, undoubtedly, a major hurdle to optimal athletic performance. Most experts believe that self-confidence can be learned and improved and that possessing resilient confidence is an essential component of superior athletic success.[2]

Athletes often fall into the trap of seeking confidence externally, hoping to gain it through a coach's praise or a strong performance. This could not be more damaging to their ability to display grit. While external validation can be beneficial for short bursts of confidence, it does not develop sustainable self-confidence. I sincerely believe that true confidence is an internal journey of personal growth that can only be unlocked by the individual. It cannot be bestowed or taken away by others. In fact, we are the ones responsible for either surrendering our confidence, which results in fear and lack of competitive capability, or holding on to it, which helps us to find grit. Whether we release or keep our confidence consciously or not, we cannot blame anyone but ourselves for doing either. What I am saying is that keeping confidence is a choice we make.

Renowned Canadian basketball coach Dave Smart, a 13-time national champion, once shared with me a powerful concept about confidence. He likened it to a key that is always around our neck, and we, as the holder, have the ultimate authority to remove it. I was inspired by this metaphor and shared it with my team. I provided each player with a lanyard and a key, which symbolized the key to their confidence. I explained to them that for their confidence to be taken away, someone has to physically remove the lanyard from their neck. Unless they willingly allow someone to do so or hand over the key themselves, their confidence can never be taken away without their consent. This exercise shows the power we hold, unless we consciously surrender it.

Right before the playoffs in the season of our first national championship, one of our starters, Raelyn, was battling a crisis of self-confidence. She had a tendency to perform well in games until a referee's unfavourable call against her would trigger a cascade of negative reactions. This chain of events would lead to anger, followed by a loss of focus and ultimately a complete lack of self-belief. Recognizing this pattern, I challenged Raelyn's perspective after one of our practices. I felt she had given the referees the key to her confidence. She responded passionately that I had been the one who took her key away. Leaving me momentarily stunned, I attempted to diffuse the situation by checking my pockets reassuring her I did not have her key. I concluded that *she* must have taken the key off her neck herself and given it away. I thought I was making my point, but she shouted, "It's on the fucking floor!" I responded, "You better put it back around your neck and show up with it this weekend because it's a playoff game and we are going to need you!" Raelyn stormed out.

Raelyn's crisis of confidence initially led to an outburst, but maybe it sparked a transformative journey for her. It needed to be said that confidence is the player's responsibility. Raelyn understood this and took it upon herself to figuratively put her key back around her neck. By the playoff game that weekend, she emerged as a pivotal player, demonstrating grit and emotional control. She did not once let a referee get to her in all of our six playoff games. It was remarkable to observe. Her contributions were instrumental in securing our team's first national championship. A proud memory for me was right after she had received her gold medal, she walked past me and picked me up, threw me over her right shoulder, and said, "Coach, I think I finally love you!"

TIME-OUT

Research shows that self-confidence is a key factor in career success, helping workers reach their goals, while its absence leads others to fall short.[3] Similarity, in sports, confident athletes work harder, set more challenging goals, and persist through adversity longer. They attribute their performance to their effort, ability, and preparation—all factors within their control. In contrast, less confident athletes attribute their performance to uncontrollable factors such as chance, the opponent, or the officials.[4]

3. Traps versus Truth

Over the past several years, significant advancements in neuroscience have unveiled the remarkable capacity of the human brain to undergo structural and functional transformations. Among the methodologies discovered is the process of substituting negative automatic thoughts with positive affirmations, presenting a promising avenue for facilitating brain rewiring. In line with this scientific breakthrough, I created a rewiring chart for our athletes titled Traps versus Truth. Figure 13 is one example of a chart I gave to a player who struggled with mistake response. It distinguishes between seeking external sources of confidence and nurturing it from within. Players are encouraged to read them and repeat the truth phrases to change their thinking from negative to positive. More truth phrases can be created depending on the needs of an athlete.

A few weeks after explaining to the team the power of rewiring one's brain out of traps and into truth, one of my players came to my office for a meeting. She looked happy, and as she opened her binder, I saw that she had created a full page of her own with traps versus truth, something she called her "affirmations." She read the affirmations every morning when she woke up to start her day well and in the right mindset. Someone who does not have a positive mindset about themselves or who has a negative mistake response cannot display grit. An additional benefit of rewiring our

TRAP		TRUTH
If you find yourself thinking ...		*Stop! Instead think this ...*
• The coach holds my confidence	➡	• I hold the key to my confidence
• People/moments take away my confidence	➡	• I give my confidence to others or moments
• Success gives me confidence	➡	• Confidence brings me success
• I am nothing without the approval of others	➡	• I am wonderful as I am
• I am defined by what I do	➡	• I am defined by who I am
• I need praise to feel good	➡	• I feel good and can praise myself

Figure 13: Traps versus Truths

brains in this way is the self-realization of accountability and the empowerment to take control of one's path and destiny.

> ## TIME-OUT
> Research shows that the nervous tissue in the human brain is highly adaptable to change. This characteristic, known as neuroplasticity, refers to the brain's ability to reorganize its structure and connections based on thoughts or stimuli. It wasn't until the mid- to late 20th century that researchers found that the brain remains adaptable well into adulthood.[5]

4. The Simulator

The coaching profession has evolved, and certain behaviours that were once considered motivational or strict are now perceived as intimidating. It is crucial to adapt and modernize coaching methods and create a safe environment for developing mental toughness and grit.

To impart this, we have designated three areas within our training facility: the Brave Zone, the Safe Zone, and the No Zone. The Brave Zone represents the basketball court, where our most rigorous training takes place. When players step onto the court to compete, they are confronted by opponents whose sole purpose is to defeat them. As a war metaphor would suggest, the consequences of defeat are significant. It is unacceptable to lack effort and determination in this zone. During practice, players willingly enter the Brave Zone, which means competing in drills, knowing that no one will rescue them in challenging situations. They must maintain composure and find the inner strength to overcome obstacles in pursuit of victory.

If the demands of the Brave Zone are overwhelming, a player has the option to remove themself from the intensity and seek solace in the Safe Zone. The Safe Zone is located off the court, typically on the sideline, where athletes can retreat for a moment of rest and support. It serves as a refuge for players who may feel on the brink of surrender or who are experiencing emotional distress. This practice emphasizes the importance of self-awareness and the need for personal time-outs. By recognizing their own emotional states and taking a moment to evaluate and regroup, athletes develop valuable skills in self-control and emotional resilience. In the Safe Zone, everyone, especially the coach, provides nurturing and positive reinforcement.

Before we implemented this technique, many athletes struggled with emotional outbursts, mental fatigue, and an inability to regain focus when overwhelmed. Some attributed their struggles to a "bad day," the coach, or an injury, when in reality it was that they had passed their personal threshold and were unable to self-regulate and bounce back from failure. Now, when in the Safe Zone, athletes are praised for demonstrating self-awareness and managing their limits. We stand beside them, offering encouragement, and when they are ready, they can rejoin the training on their own terms. With practice, they can make the transition back to being competitive.

Lastly, we have a designated area called the No Zone, which is our team room. It is available for players who are not ready to participate in any of the practice activities that day. We have never had a player choose to remain in the No Zone, but if they do one day, it will be respected, and they will be welcomed to join practice when they are ready.

The Simulator is a term we use to describe drills designed to mimic pressure moments during game play in the Brave Zone. These pressures are physical (being out of breath, overpowered), mental (being distracted by a crowd, being flustered by mistakes, losing a lead), or emotional (feeling something is unfair, losing composure). The key is to set up parameters beforehand and give players the choice to participate in the drill or not—this is how we attempt to create a safe environment to teach grit. Partaking in the Simulator is a mutual agreement in which the player agrees to be pushed with pressure. Players understand that these drills will put them through tough physical, mental, and emotional overloads. Eventually, a player reaches a threshold point, and as we discussed earlier in the book, that threshold is exactly what they must learn to overcome. Players may fail, and those failures are likely to bring up an array of emotions and expose more of their weaknesses. The goal is for these exercises to eventually unleash their ability to bounce back and prevail or to push their threshold points further. Those are breakthrough moments.

I remember one such moment for one of our best scorers. She agreed to partake in the Simulator in scrimmage, and we had mutually agreed that she would not know what pressures would be thrown at her. We wanted to increase her ability to perform on the court with weaker teammates, so we created a scrimmage where she was on a team with our weakest players, intentionally setting up a challenging situation for her. The scrimmage started, and she did not play hard, seemingly demotivated by being on a weak team. Eventually, she asked for a sub, and her team lost. In the Safe Zone, she realized this had been her Simulator exercise, and she asked for another chance and led her team with determination. Although they didn't win, they improved significantly, losing 5–4 instead of 5–0. After practice, she thanked me and left with a smile, proud of her growth and accomplishments. She became the leader and point guard she knew she needed to be, independent of whom she played with.

We do not always use the Simulator for drills, but when we do, it puts the onus on the players to find ways to cope and develop strategies to overcome their weaknesses. It also builds a long-term, healthy relationship between players and coaches through trust. It is one of our best strategies for enhancing our players' grit and their desire to improve.

5. Distributing Power

Growth is an inherent part of life's journey. It is of utmost importance that the young women in our program have ample opportunities to develop their decision-making and leadership abilities. By adopting a power distribution approach, we shift the emphasis from ourselves as coaches to them as players. Sharing power with players was a fundamental element of how we won championships because the players were emboldened to make strong on-court decisions.

As you may recall in previous chapters, Miah-Marie posed a coaching challenge for me. From my perspective, she appeared to be unresponsive to my coaching. In the first few years, I thought the only way to get through to her was to try to break her, like taming a wild horse. Regrettably, this tactic only worsened our coach-athlete relationship, and I suggested she consult with our mental performance coach (MPC) to help with the situation. That approach didn't yield a positive response either. I was puzzled as to how to reach her. Over time, I noticed that even though she didn't listen to me, she listened to others. The more I observed her, the more I realized that she had a rather easy relationship with each of my assistant coaches, which irritated me. One day it occurred to me that maybe the problem was me. What if I didn't have the skill set necessary in my leadership style to coach her effectively? This was a pivotal revelation, and I checked myself in with our MPC. Yes, after years of directing players to improve their own behaviour, I found myself in the chair, seeking advice. Our MPC proposed a strategy inspired by the renowned Duke University head coach Mike Krzyzewski. The approach was straightforward: if I couldn't effectively communicate with an athlete because she was resistant to my instruction, I needed to deliver the message through someone she listened to, specifically another player. What mattered was not who was calling the shots, but that our team was headed in the same direction. The focus of distributing power is on the goals being met, rather than anyone seeking personal power from being credited for the outcome.

When thinking about how to manage this, I decided to reach out to Anna, that same player who, through intervening in one of our game time-outs, had us won a playoff game. Her intuition and intelligence had everyone on the team respecting her, including Miah-Marie. Anna became my proxy to coach her. If I needed Miah-Marie to do something on the floor, I would pass the message through Anna who would somehow get the point across. It was like magic: we finally had Miah-Marie playing the way we needed.

What made this approach even more remarkable was that Anna, as a bench player, now had an extra role on the team that enabled her to feel a sense of importance and value. The power dynamics changed, with a clear distribution of power from me to her, benefitting Anna and the entire team. My relationship with Miah-Marie also shifted towards accomplishing tasks rather than engaging in power struggles. In the end, the team's collective performance improved, and everyone's mental strength, self-control, and grit did too.

TIME-OUT

Research on serial winning coaches reveals a common trait: driven benevolence. This is defined as "the purposeful and determined pursuit of excellence, grounded in a lasting and balanced commitment to supporting both oneself and others." These coaches focus on empowering their athletes and prefer to share decision-making responsibilities.[6]

CHAPTER 14

Striving for Mastery

"Mastery is not a destination; it is a journey. The true master is never complacent, always seeking to learn and grow, continuously refining their skills and pushing the boundaries of what is possible."

—GEORGE LEONARD

George Leonard was an American author, educator, and martial artist known for his writings on personal growth, human potential, and the pursuit of mastery. Mastery involves embracing the process of learning and continuous improvement until success is reached. Leonard's books explore the concept of mastery as a transformative journey rather than a destination. Of course, it cannot be reached unless one has developed a high level of perseverance and grit.

A MASTER OF MASTERY

In the world of professional basketball, one coach stands out as a true master of teaching grit and performance through team chemistry: Phil Jackson. Known as the "Zen Master," Jackson is best known for coaching the Chicago Bulls, beginning in the late 1980s. From the start, he displayed a unique approach that combined basketball strategy with mindfulness and psychology. Jackson embraced a holistic coaching philosophy that went beyond the Xs and Os, focusing on building a strong team culture and fostering individual growth. He led the Chicago Bulls to six NBA championships in the 1990s, with superstar Michael Jordan as the centrepiece of the team. Jackson's ability to manage the egos and personalities of his players while instilling a sense of unity and shared purpose was unparalleled. He created an environment of trust where players felt empowered to contribute their unique skills and talents to the team's success. In *Sacred Hoops*, Jackson writes,

> I flashed back to 1989 when I took over as head coach and had talked to Michael about how I wanted him to share the spotlight with his teammates so the team could grow and flourish. In those days he . . . had to be cajoled into making sacrifices for the team. Now he was an older, wiser player who understood that it wasn't brilliant individual performances that made great teams, but the energy that's unleashed when players put their ego aside and work towards a common goal.[1]

After leaving the Bulls, Jackson took on the challenge of coaching the Los Angeles Lakers. With a new roster of talented players, including Kobe Bryant and Shaquille O'Neal, Jackson continued his winning ways. Under his guidance, the Lakers won five NBA championships between 2000 and 2010, solidifying Jackson's legacy as one of the greatest coaches in basketball history. What set Jackson apart was his ability to adapt his coaching style to fit the needs of different players and teams. He was a master of identifying and nurturing the strengths of his athletes, while also challenging them to overcome their weaknesses. Jackson believed in the power of mindfulness and introduced meditation practices into his coaching approach, helping players find mental clarity and focus amid the pressures of the game. His legacy serves as an inspiration for coaches around the world, showcasing the transformative power of mastering the art and science of coaching.

MY PURSUIT OF MASTERY

My own personal coaching philosophy is rooted in the pursuit of mastery of my craft. As such, I read Phil Jackson's books to learn more about how I could emulate his coaching greatness. The one area that has by far demanded most of my attention has been learning to find the balance between pushing individuals to perform while developing strong, meaningful coach-player relationships.

> ## TIME-OUT
> The research is clear: a positive coach-athlete relationship influences athlete performance outcomes and is a crucial element for success in a high-performance sport environment. A positive coach-athlete relationship is defined as a situation where the coach's and athlete's feelings, thoughts, and behaviours are interdependent. The relationship is considered interdependent if the athlete experiences high levels of respect and trust, intends to remain attached and committed to the relationship, and behaves in a responsive, friendly, and easygoing manner.[2]

When I took over as head coach of Windsor in 2005, I was committed to building relationships, but my focus was more transactional than transformational. My goal-oriented personality overlooked and sometimes cast a shadow on a player's need for connection. To me, coach-athlete relationships were moulded on the court; they needed to be positive and reflect a business-like mindset so I could make the tough decisions needed for our culture and to achieve results. It was not something that I thought needed to be emphasized off the court. While I remained approachable and would always make a point to get to know my players, I have to admit that sometimes I failed to provide the consistent human connection my players looked for. As time passed, I saw my profession as a whole move towards an athlete-centred model of coaching. For me, a pivotal moment was a morning breakfast encounter with a player's father.

In my third year at Windsor, I had convinced Emily Abbott, a 17-year-old, to leave home and move halfway across the country to play for us. She had an outgoing personality, but we quickly discovered that she was extremely homesick. Like most players her age, she lacked the coping skills that would have made her transition to living on her own easier. She was my first player who had come from far away, so we spent a lot of time helping and listening to her. In other words, we had to invest in her growth as a person if we ever hoped to see her perform on the court. Over the years, she matured and transformed. Her confidence grew to the point that we named her captain in her final year. During that year, Emily played the best basketball we had seen her play in her five years. She was physical, decisive, and in a high-performing state all season. As luck would have it, the national championship was hosted in her hometown in her last year, and it brings me great joy to know that Emily got to experience winning in front of her family and friends.

At the end of her varsity career, her father, who had been in the Canadian Air Force, invited me for breakfast. While I was eating with Emily's parents, her father shared with me how elated he was at the progress Emily had made in basketball and how joyful he was for our national titles. When he proceeded to thank me for taking care of his daughter over the last five years, he suddenly went silent and bowed his head. His wife put her hand on his. When he raised his head back up, he said in a trembling voice, "I wanted to thank you. Five years ago, I gave you a child; five years later, you brought me back a woman." I had rarely heard something so meaningful. We had just clinched the national trophy, but this was not nearly as important to him. What was important was who Emily had become, not what she had done. For a person like me, who traditionally had been focused on results, this was nothing short of mind-blowing. That connection I had established with Emily was meaningful to her as well; she had summarized her experience of our relationship to the local newspaper as "Coach is a hard ass with a big heart."

My experience with Emily encouraged me to become a lot more people-oriented in my approach from that point on. However, this did not always yield the results I was hoping for. Players often had a hard time understanding why I would make a tough business decision when "we just had such a great chat," or why I would sit them out of a game saying they were not ready when I promoted growth and time to adapt. When I focused almost solely on my personal relationships, the pendulum swung too far towards a personal transformational focus, and I had to bring it back. I realized that, like everything else, operating at the centre was not the sweet spot. Mastery relied in the ability to move along the spectrum between being result-driven and people-driven as each circumstance presented itself, and in the ability to discern what to emphasize in each instance. A coach's daily job is to make decisions that both gain results and build relationships, to focus on outcomes and people, to take actions of transaction and transformation.

Transactional leadership involves drawing the line on behaviours, cutting a player, making a substitution, choosing to take a time-out, or suspending a team member. This leadership style is essential because it breeds compliance and sets clear expectations and standards with the aim to maximize results. It adds the necessary structure. This is well illustrated in military hierarchy. There is no room for negotiation because many decisions must be made quickly and under pressure. Transactional leadership organizes the team and enhances short-term group performance.

On the other hand, a transformational leader's work is capable of motivating followers by moving them towards a shared vision. It engages creativity and accountability, while cultivating leadership skills. It helps people and the organization to grow and change. It fosters life skills development and a positive engaging team culture. Problems arise when a coach sticks to one leadership style when the situation calls for the other. Finding a balance is key. Too much transactional focus can erode the meaningful relationships that make coaching human, turning it into a purely business-oriented model. Conversely, excessive transformational emphasis can lead to a lack of direction and clarity. It's important to maintain both styles and know when to employ each one effectively. Figure 14 depicts the movement of these two leadership styles over the years and where I believe the next twenty years are headed.

Pre-2000s	2000–2020	2020s+
• Task-oriented	• People-oriented	• Task and people-oriented
• Dictatorship	• Empowerment	• Caring authoritarian
• About me	• About them	• About us
• Physical focus	• Mental/emotional focus	• Spiritual focus
• Push physical limits	• Train mental	• Centering, meditation
• Coach holds all power	performance	• Coach distributes power
• Transaction	• Players challenge the	• Transaction &
• Coach's voice	power	transformation
	• Transformation	• Our voice
	• Player's voice	

Figure 14: How Coaching Has Changed over Time

HOLISTIC COACHING

As the landscape of leadership and coaching continues to evolve, a more comprehensive approach has emerged. Holistic coaching not only addresses an individual's performance but also nurtures their personal growth, helping them thrive in all areas of life. Holistic coaching recognizes that we are more than just the roles we play or our job title—we are individuals with personal experiences, aspirations, and potential that extends far beyond the immediate task at hand.

The roots of holistic coaching can be traced back to the mid-20th century when companies and organizations began to recognize the importance of employee well-being and started offering health and wellness programs. In the early 1990s, the holistic health movement gained momentum, and coaching began to shift from a narrow focus on results to a broader, more integrated, nurturing approach.

Holistic coaching, much like transformational leadership, emphasizes the long-term development of the individual, but with an added focus on health, relationships, career, and emotional well-being. It combines elements of both transactional and transformational leadership but goes deeper, addressing all aspects of an individual's life, from their physical health to their personal relationships, and from their emotional resilience to their spiritual growth.

In sports, holistic coaching empowers athletes to take ownership of their decisions and actions, both on and off the field. It's not just about coaching them to win; it's about equipping them to lead and make meaningful contributions to their teams. In business and education, this same philosophy applies: when leaders foster an environment where individuals feel supported and valued in all areas of their lives, they are more likely to thrive. This holistic approach leads to greater engagement, collaboration, and innovation because individuals are not just working toward a shared goal—they feel personally connected to it.

THE PROGRESSION TOWARDS COACHING MASTERY

John Wooden, a legendary basketball coach, is often considered an early prophet of holistic coaching. Wooden mastered both transformational and transactional leadership so well that he has been my greatest inspiration for mastering balance. He won ten national basketball championships for UCLA by emphasizing extreme discipline for his players, including how to properly wear socks. Yet when asked about his core values, he was quick to explain that his goal was to develop each individual's personal skills first and their athletic skills second. Wooden is known as much for his on-court success as he is for the off-court success of his players. He has said, "What you are as a person is far more important than what you are as a basketball player." NBA Hall of Famer Kareem Abdul-Jabbar, arguably Wooden's most successful basketball player, described his college coach's leadership style like this:

> It's kind of hard to talk about Coach Wooden because he was a very complex man, but he taught in a very simple way. He used sports to teach us how to apply ourselves to any situation. He set quite an example. He was more of a parent than a coach. He was a very selfless and giving individual, but he was a disciplinarian.

In his book *They Call Me Coach*, Wooden writes, "I often told my players that, next to my own flesh and blood, they were the closest to me. They were my children. I became deeply involved in their lives and their problems."[3] What I appreciate even more about Wooden is how he defined success as "peace of mind, which comes from self-satisfaction in knowing you did your best to become the best that you are capable of becoming."[4] From this perspective, Wooden's definition of success aligns closely with the philosophy of most, if not all, of the expert coaches we interviewed as part of our research.

Exploring Wooden's approach continued to engage my own reflection on leadership, character, and mastery in all aspects of coaching and leading. Reflecting upon how I progressed in my own coaching career, through different sports, levels, and with different genders, I created the following Progression of Coaching concept. I have used it as barometer to identify where I stand and what to aim for next.

Balancing a leadership equilibrium between a deep investment in players' personal growth and tough coaching calls for the sake of

APPRENTICE COACH	ESTABLISHED COACH	WINNING COACH	MASTER COACH
• somewhat new or a few years into coaching • searching for coaching voice/leadership style • building own coaching philosophy • lacking depth of experience in the coaching profession • needing to learn more about the technical, tactical, physical, mental aspects	• common type of coach considered successful because of long career, usually 10 years + • professional and knowledgeable • keeps team in good standing • gets the job done	• wins regularly • produces winning seasons • remain a constant presence among the top rankings • undergone a personal transformation • recovers quickly from mistakes • good mentor • wins championships • may develop professionals or Olympians	• multiple championship wins • termed "serial winning coaches" • considered gurus • have long careers • seldom make mistakes • have leadership equilibrium • examples: Phil Jackson, John Wooden, Pat Summitt

Figure 15: The Progression of Coaching

performance has been a real challenge. And it gets trickier with each new generation of players. On one hand, coaching demands finesse, knowing that success isn't only about winning games. On the other, coaches' careers often hinge on team performance—it's all about those wins and losses. Effective coaches see beyond scores, valuing players' growth and resilience. Yet a winning program needs a coach who ignites both a competitive spirit and a winning record. This has been one of the trickiest equilibriums for me to master. At times, I have felt I went too far in pushing the players. At other times, I went home thinking I was getting too soft, and I worried that I was making it seem like the easy way out was okay. As time has passed, I have mostly felt stuck between realizing that my players need to learn about resiliency and the reality that I cannot teach this to them by pushing them over the edge. Mastering this balance is an ongoing process.

One of my proudest moments in finding the right balance, moving towards mastery, and fostering holistic coaching came during our journey to winning our fourth national championship. I was eager to implement a grit-boosting technique by distributing power as widely as possible. This championship provided the perfect opportunity, as our two best players were graduating, and they had already secured three national titles. As we entered the playoff season, I gradually stepped back from leading as much as I could, focusing instead on empowering the players to take charge. I must have succeeded, because a couple of years later one of my players mentioned that she felt I hadn't done much during those final championship games—and she was right! Although

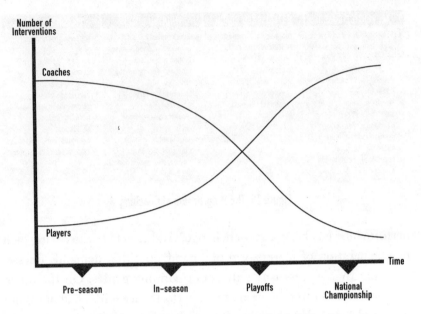

Figure 16: The Distributing Power Model of Coaching

she may not have realized it was intentional, this experience inspired me to develop a diagram (Figure 16) illustrating my belief that a coach should be highly involved at the start of the season, early in a player's career, or when the team is young. Over time as the playoffs approach, a rookie evolves into a senior, or the team matures, the coach should gradually distribute more power and responsibility to the players, intervening much less. In essence, a full distribution of power signifies that the coach has successfully completed the transformation necessary for the players to take the reins of the team. The coach remains in a role of support and encouragement and provides occasional strategic direction and transactional decisions during preparation and games.

Today's players want to understand the why behind everything we do as coaches. To help them embrace an approach that is more coach-led at the beginning, I often use Figure 16 to explain why we frequently stop drills and scrimmages early in the season, a decision that is unpopular with the players. When players understand that these pauses are essential for building the systems we want in place, they become more open to this method and look forward to us stepping back and trusting them to take the lead.

This figure also serves as a constant reminder for me to gradually distribute power to the players as the seasons—and their careers—progress. It keeps me accountable for fostering grit in my players by stepping back and relinquishing control as they mature. This approach allows them to self-correct and reduces the need for my interventions during practices and games. Almost every time, players respond, and in the case of our fourth national title, a veteran team of players led us to victory on their own.

GOING FOR THE LAST KILL

Even though all of our championship wins share similar coaching elements, including overcoming adversity, finding grit, and going for the kill by performing at the right time, progress in our coaching and our experience also played a role. It was not until we were an established coaching staff that we were able to lead the team to the successful climb of Everest and win our first title. As we attempted to summit K2, our second mountain climb, we committed to our ongoing personal development as players and staff. By the time the third championship came around, it brought its own set of new challenges. We played the national final against the University of Regina, a team that was not only experienced in the finals but had the benefit of playing on their home court. Regina's colour is green, and unfortunately the national final happened to be on St. Patrick's Day. We woke up that morning to an entire city wearing green, tailgating, and cheering unimaginably loud, as thousands of fans entered the gym to see a hometown win. That year, our climb was the Cordillera de los Llanganates in Ecuador. The goal was to summit some of the most dangerous active volcanos and find the gold of old buried Inca treasure. I compared the imminent support for the other team to volcanic explosions on our path: be ready. Our pre-game speech emphasized that this was our last trek and that the treasure was close. I urged our players not to become distracted by external disturbances and to continue their quest with a strengthened sense of togetherness.

We led by a small margin throughout the first half. We took a considerable lead in the third quarter, but then Regina began a comeback in the fourth quarter. With about six minutes to go in the game, one of their post players nailed a game-changing three-pointer to take the lead. We had lost all momentum. I clearly remember the deafening sound in the gym. Even though the energy had become overwhelming, two of my veterans remained stoic and took it upon themselves to lead the charge back. In our final time-out, I stood by as they reminded us all that it was the volcano erupting and to stay focused: "This is the lightning and thunder that Coach warned us about." I nodded and did not add anything tactical to the time-out. I urged everyone to stay focused on our three-point game plan, and everyone nodded. My colleague spoke up: "Go and finish the climb: you want to get there, and most importantly you know how to get there." My colleague's advice had come in very handy in this critical moment, and this motivating vote of confidence was all my players needed to hear. The team went back on the floor and took back the lead. We won our third national championship against a host team and their hostile crowd.

The key was that the players spoke up and took over as leaders, not me. I didn't have to take control. These players had become accustomed to "killing it," and in my own progression of coaching, I had established a positive leadership equilibrium by letting them do it.

As I mentioned earlier, the fourth title was all about distributing power. I chose Denali not because of its height but because of its steepness. To highlight this, I pulled aside our two captains, Miah-Marie and Jessica Clemençon, and asked them before we started our playoff run, "Tell me honestly, do you think that if you play your best"—I pointed at Miah-Marie—"and you play your best"—I pointed at Jessica—"that you can lose to anyone?" They both looked at each other and smiled. "No." "Right! Then you lead the team this time," I said. They had seen me lead the team for three years, and I felt it was time to empower them and give them the reins. They left the office somewhat confident; however, I am not sure any of us knew what this would look like. I watched as they excitedly prepared the team by organizing meetings before practices. They poured over scouting reports and reviewed with everyone. They also raised their game by including everyone in their praise and rallying the troops every chance they could, from the floor and from the bench. They showed up as individual players and played their strongest basketball, peaking at the right time for their last year of eligibility. They led us to the national championship finals, where we played St. Mary's University, a team that had been undefeated and boasted a player on the senior women's national team. In a dominating fashion, we took a lead of 40–14. St Mary's was never in the game, and we won 71–45. I wish there was more roller-coaster excitement to this story, but in reality, our leaders killed their task and were merciless

Now, I could not have written better what happened next. Unbeknownst to me, the following year's national championship was set to be hosted in the province of Quebec, the place I grew up in and call home. It was in Quebec City that I experienced this momentous occasion. My friends and family had gathered to witness me coaching, culminating a journey that had started ten years earlier when I had left them to venture into a new culture and language. I had returned home with a team that was missing key players who had been injured during the off-season. With only eight players at our disposal, we faced a serious challenge in this Elite Eight tournament. To supplement our depleted roster, we outfitted our team manager in a uniform so we could say we had nine. Despite these setbacks, throughout the season, we had learned to persevere, and our trials had forged a group of indomitable women, prepared to kill when it truly counted.

As I had contemplated the theme for this season, the idea had struck me to take the team on another expedition to Mount Everest. This majestic mountain held a special place for two of our fifth-year players, Korissa and Jocelyn, who had conquered it in a much lesser role as rookies five years ago. However, they had seen their vets lead and win, and they knew the path; they knew how to tackle it. It was now their time to be leaders. Returning to Everest became a powerful motivator and a source of self-confidence for them. After all, they had already achieved this feat once, and since then, they had gone on to win four championships. They had witnessed their senior teammates and captains lead the way the previous year, and now it was their turn. What made it even more extraordinary was the opportunity to make history by winning five consecutive national titles. It would distinguish them as the only two women ever to accomplish such a remarkable feat. It would also provide them with a sense of closure, marking the perfect ending to their careers by coming back to the mountain where they started it all.

The completion of the circle was also truly a fitting end to my journey, almost like something out of a Hollywood movie. In the final match, we faced off against McGill University, my alma mater. It was the place where it had all started, the place where I had completed my master's degree and learned the art of turning around struggling programs and building championship teams through my thesis research. McGill had played a pivotal role in shaping my career, ultimately leading me to become the head coach at Windsor. I was filled with a sense of fulfillment and gratitude before the final game.

No one expected us to win, because we had lost Miah-Marie and Jessica—our two all-Canadians and two of the best players ever to wear a Lancer uniform. In spite of this, my fifth-year veterans made it happen by playing almost the entire game to go for one final kill. As the final seconds counted down and I saw we were in the lead, I remember feeling quite emotional. When I felt the tears running down my cheeks, I hugged and hid in the arms of my two burly assistant coaches, who were about six-foot-seven and 250 pounds each. I could not believe we had won. I could not believe we had done it *again*.

The only other time I had been slightly emotional at a championship was the first one, in 2011. Five seasons later, we had just equalled a record of five championships in a row—a record held only by the Laurentian women's university team in the mid-1970s. In the moment, the record was not important to me, and though the title was certainly fantastic, nothing was on my mind more than the fact that I was home. It had been daring for me to leave the comfort of my culture and language ten years earlier on a quest to turn a losing program into a national champion. Just like the leaders I had studied and modelled myself after—Sylvie Bernier, Gary Barnett, Walt Disney, John Wooden—my vision had come true and more than once . . . It had far exceeded what I had imagined when creating the Lancers's five-year plan.

That winning day stands out as one of the most significant moments in my career and pursuit of coaching mastery. The team from my alma mater, McGill University, the very team we had just defeated, formed a line in front of us. As I watched them applaud, it felt as though they were figuratively saying, "You came from here, we played a part in your journey, and we are proud of your success." My gaze then shifted to the stands filled with my loved ones. They stood there, beaming with pride as we lifted the Bronze Baby trophy. It was as if they, too, were calling out to me, saying, "You come from here. We also played a role in shaping your path." As we were introduced as the national champions in French, my mother tongue, a euphoric feeling swept over me. It was like a gentle nudge from the universe, affirming that I had chosen the right path and that all the sacrifices had been worthwhile. Yes, I was a winning coach, but more importantly, I had become a better person through this journey. I felt a deep sense of gratitude that basketball had allowed me to explore and uncover my true self, encouraging vulnerability and fostering personal growth.

NEXT PLAY

When I had started my research at McGill, I did not know much about vision, mission, values, or managing, and even less about mindfulness, the pressure coaches feel in the face of leading a group of people, and the necessity to teach grit to win. But I knew that I wanted to be a great coach and reach new heights of success. This desire was the start of my career vision and mission. Once I got into coaching, I hit many roadblocks and the lessons I learned forced me to re-evaluate myself. When I started winning, I felt validated and I wanted to stay on top forever, which, of course, doesn't seem to be possible for any of us! Yet, having won for five years in a row, it had almost become a lifestyle for me. As you can imagine, when my team went through normal cycles of rebuilding after the five-peat, when we had to work hard to reach the top again, I got caught up in solely wanting to win. Despite all the knowledge I had acquired through my research and experience at Windsor, I was used to winning, and I was not okay with having to be patient. I did not remember that it takes a lot of time for a new generation of players to understand and learn all about grit and grind. I demanded instant results, and for a few years, I lost my way. It is through writing this book that I was able to truly appreciate the entire process. I became re-invigorated and dedicated myself to coaching a new crop of athletes to the same heights I have experienced. I have made a commitment to strive for one final ascent towards the mastery of coaching. I've made a pledge to dedicate the rest of my life to honing my skills as a coach and making a positive impact on others for the sake of the journey, not the destination. And so I want to share with you principles that can help beyond basketball.

Here are seven principles of mastery for life that I have found through research on successful coaches and learned through personal experience during my long career in leadership and coaching. This is what I abide by as I lead my program with renewed energy and focus.

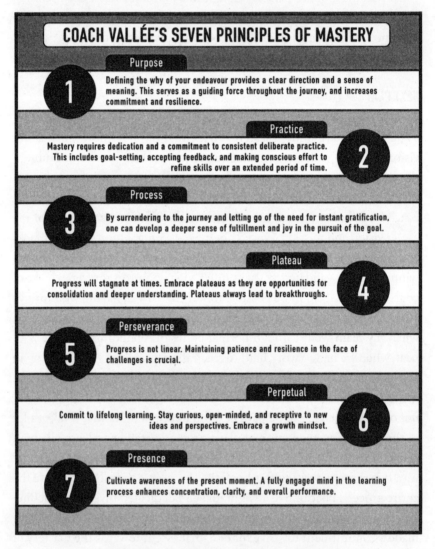

Figure 17: Coach Vallée's Seven Principles of Mastery

In striving towards mastery, I have adopted these principles in the following simple ways.

1. **Purpose:** My why is teaching others how to become excellent. In the end, this is what motivates me to continue coaching.

2. **Practice:** Every time I step on the floor with my team, I deliberately practice all the leadership and management skills contained in this book. I call this my lab.

3. **Process:** I forgot about the process part of mastery after the five-peat. I need to constantly remind myself of process-based leadership to stay on course. Once I realigned on process, I no longer felt the need for instant gratification.

4. **Plateau:** Plateaus are a part of the grind, and the best way I have learned to cope with them is to accept that they are part of the journey. Enjoy them instead of fighting them.

5. **Perseverance:** When I need to draw on perseverance, I use my own traps versus truths affirmations as well as positive self-talk to keep going.

6. **Perpetual:** Writing this book was an action of continuous learning for me; putting my knowledge and experiences on paper helped me to continue to grow and become more self-aware.

7. **Presence:** My own self-development has taught me to cultivate the present moment and to stretch myself into long hours of deep meditation. This has significantly reduced my stress, allowed me to control my emotions, and in increasing my health and well-being, has helped that of my team as well.

QUARTER BREAK

Four Keys to Mastering the Ascent

1. **DEVELOP GRIT** in your team and in yourself. Research demonstrates that grit scores the highest as a success indicator. Grit is built through physical and mental endurance and strengthened by emotional resilience, such as perseverance.

2. **SIMULATE THE ASCENT.** Winning, like climbing a mountain, is something that can be learned, developed, and refined. It's essential to engage in rigorous simulations that mimic the challenges of real competition. These high-stakes practice scenarios prepare you and your team to navigate obstacles, maintain focus, and build the skills and mindset needed to reach the summit under duress.

3. **GO FOR THE KILL.** This approach embodies absolute commitment and unwavering focus. Success often requires a do-or-die attitude. It's not about being reckless; it's about being relentless. Prepare and strategize, but when the moment comes, execute with a level of resolve that leaves no room for failure. Leave your burdens at the foot of the hill.

4. **PURSUE MASTERY.** This is the leader's ultimate quest: finding the balance between winning and growing, doing and being, achieving and regrouping, making transactions and transforming. Mastery requires a foundation of emotional health, enabling you to shift the focus from personal gain to the collective good. Leadership mastery is never fully achieved. As society evolves, it will always remain a moving target.

COACH INSIGHT: Mastery can also be applied to the science of well-being and happiness. It doesn't have to be about work, accolades, or accomplishments.

LOOK AHEAD TO OVERTIME

Can one master the research model to the point where success can be achieved more efficiently or in a different context? Keep reading to see how it became possible.

OVERTIME

"I love to see a young girl go out and grab the world by the lapels. Life's a bitch. You've got to go out and kick ass."

—MAYA ANGELOU

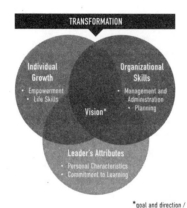

*goal and direction /
leader's philosophy

In a broader context, overtime is a metaphor for those moments in life and leadership when time is short, stakes are high, and the usual rules no longer apply. Whether in business, negotiations, or any high-pressure situation, the ability to "win in overtime" means first mastering the arts of quick thinking, decisive action, and drawing out the best in others when it matters most.

To succeed in overtime is to navigate the fine line between urgency and composure, to transform pressure into performance, and to lead a team to triumph. It's the mark of a leader who can turn a fleeting moment into a lasting victory, proving that in the end, it's not only about the time you have—but how you use it.

Time to use the research to become excellent at replicating success in other contexts—and more quickly!

CHAPTER 15

Going Pro

S uccess, like winning national championships, opens doors that I'd never before imagined. During a sabbatical in 2018–19, I relocated to Montreal for a few months to start writing this book and to be closer to Dr. Gordon Bloom's research lab at McGill University. About a month after I settled in, an interesting email landed in my inbox. John Lashway, a 22-year veteran executive in the NBA with Portland and Toronto, was reaching out to gauge my interest in becoming the head coach and general manager of a professional team in in the Toronto area. When we connected by phone, I assumed he would elaborate on plans for a WNBA team to come to Toronto. I was surprised to find out that he was talking about a men's professional basketball franchise in the newly created Canadian Elite Basketball League (CEBL).

I had never imagined coaching professional men, simply because I didn't think it was possible. Sure, I had heard of the few women coaches in the men's pro game. I had even met Nancy Lieberman, the first woman head coach of an NBA G League team in 2009, and knew of Becky Hammon, who in 2014 became the first woman to be paid as a full-time coach on an NBA staff. However, the thought had never even crossed my mind that I could be considered for a similar opportunity, especially for a head coach *and* general manager position I had not even applied for.

As soon as I hung up the phone, I researched the CEBL online. As we've learned throughout this book, any organization's ability to succeed is linked to the quality of the leadership team, which determines its vision, mission, values, and culture. I would only consider being involved if there was a clearly identified and compelling vision. The CEBL did not disappoint. It had an articulated mission that immediately got my attention, which I have summarized in Table 2 below:

Integrate	Create	Foster	Develop
Integrate communities by creating unity, pride, and economic benefits for host cities of 7 professional teams.	Create a culture of warm family-friendly environments around professional basketball by targeting smaller city hubs.	Foster Canadian basketball growth by highlighting Canadian talent and signing the top international players to play in Canada.	Develop Canadian coaches, players, referees, and front office staff through hands-on experience with professional sport.

Table 2: Canadian Elite Basketball League Vision

It seemed like a great opportunity for me to get hands-on experience in professional basketball and grow my own coaching career. For the Hamilton Honey Badgers franchise, John carried a vision that resonated with me: a dream to build a championship franchise in year one. He believed that a winning first season would foster a trickle-down effect to enhance the community of Hamilton. And he wanted to invest in front-office staff leadership development.

To many, the idea of heading up a new franchise with an inexperienced front-office staff would be enough to deter them from taking on a GM and head coach position, but to me it was incredibly attractive and challenging once-in-a-lifetime opportunity. John's NBA experience gave him an appreciation for what it takes to build an entire program and culture from nothing—especially the necessity for broader leadership skills beyond coaching basketball. John was convinced my skill set was exactly what the Honey Badgers needed to build a franchise from the ground up. His three-pronged vision for Hamilton could not have been a better fit for me. John had done his research well, and I was soon hooked on this opportunity.

MONUMENTAL TASK

After weeks of discussion between John and myself, as well as numerous collaborative meetings with the University of Windsor, I was granted the green light to work professionally for one season and still retain my position at Windsor upon my return. On November 21, 2018, I was officially named the head coach and general manager of the Hamilton Honey Badgers, making me the first woman in basketball history to be named as both the head coach and general manager of a men's professional team. I was only the second woman ever to serve as a head coach of a men's professional basketball team.

Shortly after the announcement, the internet exploded as tweets were posted by major basketball and news reporters around the world, including the WNBA, CNN and *Bleacher Report*; there were even discussions with *Sports Illustrated* about a biographical piece. The legendary Nancy Lieberman, perhaps the most iconic figure in American women's basketball, wished me good luck via Twitter. On *Sportsnet*, my name was thrown in the mix as the biggest story of the week alongside stories about LeBron James and Kevin Durant. People were responding from all over the world on social media. It was truly amazing. I had numerous interviews with major press such as the *Globe and Mail*, *The Guardian*, and other news outlets from South America to Scandinavia. All of Canada's major (and most mid-sized) media outlets covered the story.

In total, I did 24 one-on-one interviews during the 21 days after my appointment was announced, which, according to John, surpassed the media requests for any of the eight NBA head coaches he had worked alongside. It was a whirlwind of media requests and business, and for a split second, it seemed the world had stopped. I could not catch my breath, and it was a euphoric high. Then reality began to set in. What had I just gotten myself into? Without any experience or professional contacts, and with the media and CEBL focus now lying squarely on the Hamilton franchise, I look back and realize now that I was blissfully going with the flow for the first few days, believing, as John did, in my capacity to get the job done. In retrospect, it proved to be more of a challenging task than turning around the Windsor program—and I had only six months to do it.

As the dust settled, the monumental task that lay ahead of me appeared bright and clear, and I started to feel the pressure of it all weighing on my shoulders. The team did not exist. There was no structure, no players, no staff, no gym, no location to train, no systems in place, no gear to wear. More importantly, when it came to professional men's basketball, I had no contacts, no network, no leads, and no idea where to get started. I had never negotiated a player contract, talked to professional agents, or coached professional men. I did not know whom to trust, and I did not have a clue how to be a GM in the professional world. I was used to being fully focused on a roster of student-athletes and finding the right vision and role for each of them over the multiple years with our program. At the professional level, the management side felt different. As I would soon find out, professional players ask for specific concessions, including taking into consideration the needs of their spouses, time for family visits, even requesting to miss practices and in-season games for personal reasons.

The biggest challenge I had was roster building. I knew that it would be a daunting task to build a roster and sign the right players because, frankly, I was ignorant about the market. My niche was women's basketball. On that front, I was extremely well connected between my international experience as a coach on our national team, coaching professionally in South America, coaching a team of NCAA players to compete in Asia, and being at the University of Windsor. If I had to build a women's roster, it would probably have taken me one week. However, on the men's side, all I had were a few acquaintances, a handful of colleagues from opposing Canadian university teams that I would say hello to in between our double-header games, as well as American friends who had been involved in the men's NCAA as coaches or team chaplains. To make things harder, tip-off for the first game was less than six months away!

Roster building had been my only hesitation in taking the team as the GM, but I had accepted the position because the league (comprised at the time of six teams under a single-entity ownership) had planned to present a list of players with agents, phone numbers, and potential roster positions from which each GM would choose collaboratively. The initial idea was to purposely create parity in the league to make for great entertainment and secure a following. Little did I know that as the league interest grew, and other franchises began hiring competent and accomplished coaches and GMs, the competitiveness and seriousness would begin to show. As such, it was not long before this plan was abandoned, and the league decided that each GM was to build their roster on their own. As you can imagine, player procurement became the wild west as each well-connected GM began to carve out their competitive advantages in different markets and with different relationships. I was in deep trouble.

New deals were struck, and then another bomb was dropped. The league announced a professional-style draft to be held in March, only two months away, for rights to players who would be signed to contracts for the start of training camp in May. Each GM was not only in charge of player procurement but also had to partake in a draft? I remember the night when I found all this out on a call with the president of the Honey Badgers. I remember asking, "How are we going to get the players?" to which he responded, "I hired a GM for that. Find a way."

The stress level of the job quadrupled overnight. I had no clue where to start. Who were the good up-and-coming Canadian men in the pros? Who were the top international players who might be interested in spending their summer in Canada? What country should I focus on? Some of the other coaches in the league were the college or high school coaches of some of these players or assistants in other pro leagues. Some knew players from their time together with the Canadian national team or working in the NBA G League or in Europe. They could pick up a phone and get in touch with them personally or with agents rostering players in Turkey, Germany, or Korea. I didn't even know anyone's *name*. Asking me to find out and determine the best men's professionals around the world and convince them to come play in a start-up league in Hamilton, Canada, for four months in the summer was like asking a dermatologist to repair a broken tooth—yes, they're a doctor, but not the right area. My knowledge and expertise was in coaching; the transferability was easy there. It was in the business and practice of being a GM *in the men's game* that was the issue.

I had to resolve myself to managing the process the best way I knew— by slowing down my mind. I had to let ideas and images fill my brain in order to find a vision, build a strategic plan, plan a successful season, and see what that brought me in terms of daily tasks to manage. I reverted to my research and all I had learned about building a championship program. I concentrated my knowledge to execute in six months what it took me six years to build with the University of Windsor. I had no choice but to commit fully.

TIME-OUT

According to research, few positions are as multifaceted and demanding as a sport's general manager. The role of the general manager is the toughest job in professional sports due to the many responsibilities and pressures inherent within the position. From implementing a vision to hiring the support staff and building a winning team, the GM must find a way to create alignment throughout the entire organization.[1] Comparisons are made to the role of a CEO in a business, particularly how in both roles strategies are implemented to create a culture of excellence.[2]

CHAPTER 16

The Process

I went all in. Before I could even think about coaching, I had to fulfill my GM duties, and since I did not know how to go about this side of the business, I immediately sought advice where I could. I started by making a list of all the people I knew from the men's game and the professional world. My first call was to Olga Hrycak, a Canadian basketball Hall of Famer head coach who, as a woman, had successfully won several championships and Coach of the Year awards. Not only had she been coaching men successfully at a Canadian university and college level for years, but she had a few players still playing professionally overseas or involved in the game. Among them was Prosper Karangwa, then vice-president of scouting for the Orlando Magic of the NBA. (He since took a position as the vice-president of player personnel for the Philadelphia 76ers.) She put us in touch that day.

First, I was impressed by how quickly Prosper got back to me: "I will do anything for Olga; she changed my life. How can I help you, Chantal?" The respect he had for his college head coach was endearing and reassuring to me in many ways. Prosper was great and gave me the name of a person he said was the "best agent in the business for Canadian talent." "Give him a call and say, 'Prosper sent you.'" I googled this agent and quickly found out that he was the owner of one of the biggest agencies, representing many of Canada's NBA players. I wondered how receptive he would be to my call. Thankfully, connections and networking are key in getting anyone's attention, so with Prosper's backing, the call went very smoothly, and this agent became a big help for my draft preparation. I now had a few names of players, and most importantly, I had been successful in my first call to an agent, opening a tangible contract negotiation for the point guard I wanted.

As I continued in the business, I found out which agents seemed to have better players than others, which were easier to reach than others, and which ones were more eager to help than others. I had a small insider's view of how it worked in terms of discussing and negotiating contracts and salaries with the pros. I still had to find a way to connect with some players directly, and most agents were not willing to let that happen as they were extremely protective of their players' privacy.

After a few weeks, John put me in touch with Maurizio Gherardini, the very successful GM of Fenerbahçe in Istanbul. This top EuroLeague team boasted former NBA (and Canadian star) player Tyler Ennis, who was recovering from a leg injury. Maurizio spent a generous amount of time giving me advice, and we considered having Tyler rehab with us in Hamilton. Everything was moving fast, and since I was still on sabbatical travelling in Australia and New Zealand at the time, I seized the opportunity to add "meeting with professional club GMs" as part of my professional development Down Under. I was pleasantly surprised that there were a lot of people in Australia and New Zealand willing to help. The GM of the Brisbane Bullets gave me his Excel spreadsheet and showed me how to keep track of player salaries and the cap space using embedded formulas. I took so many notes, and I remember dreaming about it most nights. In the end, nothing really prepared me more than getting my hands dirty in the work itself. Finding a way, in this sense, was much about formulating questions, asking for help, finding answers, and establishing connections.

As I was getting more acquainted with the work of the GM, I was simultaneously focusing on my process of success: working at establishing a plan to build this franchise from the ground up. Referring to my coaching process, I created the skeleton for the first two sections—vision and strategic plan—in order to bring clarity to what would build a successful franchise.

As you can see, the Honey Badgers vision that I created for my one-year stint was a much more condensed version of my vision for

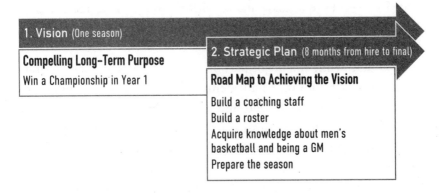

Figure 18: Hamilton Honey Badgers Coaching Process (Steps 1 and 2)

coaching the Lancers. I was hired to build a team that wins a championship in the first year of the league, and it was quite possibly my only year in this role because of my University of Windsor obligations. In retrospect, working this way was very difficult, considering the time it takes to properly develop a vision, build a culture, communicate it, and share it with others. In the end, I had to take some shortcuts and think and act in a different way. For example, with regard to roster building, there would be no extended effort towards long-term planning, such as stashing away draft choices or choosing players with long-term potential and growth. Every choice, decision, and plan had to be focused on the here and now. I knew, however, that with great planning and preparation, the team would be built on a solid foundation, and that would help the franchise succeed for years to come, which made me feel better. Long-term growth had always been a personal value that both John and I held on to dearly, and it was important that the franchise be left with important building blocks to continue towards long-term success. However, for now, that goal had to be secondary. Most immediately, the question was "How can I design a road map to build a winning team?" My initial focus was clear: "Win a championship in year one." The players, the coaches, the culture, and the strategy used had to lead to this vision. To win, I needed to convince the best players to play for us at the right part of our season, considering some were still playing in Europe or would have to leave us early for their next season. I then needed to negotiate a salary figure with their agents, to receive each player's verbal commitment to join us if we drafted them, and to finally get their signature on a contract.

Of course, while the major part of my energy was focused on draft day and roster building, I had identified three additional pillars to be assembled: building a solid and experienced staff, increasing my knowledge of coaching professional men, and planning a competitive training camp and pre-season schedule. Unlike what I did in Windsor, I did not create a full-on strategic business plan. This time around, to be more efficient and focused, I created a plan that had simple bullet points highlighting the key areas to be worked on within each of the four road map pillars.

Each one of these four pillars was vital for the vision's success and as a key contributing area in culture building. I knew the team culture

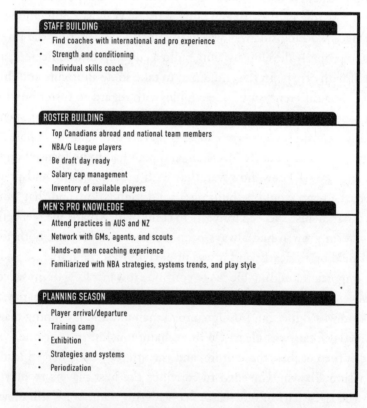

STAFF BUILDING
- Find coaches with international and pro experience
- Strength and conditioning
- Individual skills coach

ROSTER BUILDING
- Top Canadians abroad and national team members
- NBA/G League players
- Be draft day ready
- Salary cap management
- Inventory of available players

MEN'S PRO KNOWLEDGE
- Attend practices in AUS and NZ
- Network with GMs, agents, and scouts
- Hands-on men coaching experience
- Familiarized with NBA strategies, systems trends, and play style

PLANNING SEASON
- Player arrival/departure
- Training camp
- Exhibition
- Strategies and systems
- Periodization

Figure 19: Road Map to Build a Championship Franchise in Year One

would be critical; it was terrifyingly unknown until the start of the season, which left us little time to correct. Since vision and culture are intrinsically linked, the four pillars needed to be taken into consideration jointly for any decision about building the franchise. I decided to start with my own team around me, as GM and coach. With staff building, I identified that I needed to find coaches with international and professional experience. It was going to be a daunting task to work with paid professional players coming in to play for four months and to get them to buy in to me, my style, and my desired culture—especially since I had never coached professional men and the franchise culture was completely new. A strong and cohesive coaching staff was critical for strengthening my message at all levels of the road map.

TIME-OUT

In an attempt to understand cultural transformation in the elite sport environment, six owners and general managers from the NBA, MLB, and NFL who had successfully led their programs through organizational culture change were interviewed. All of these successful sport leaders developed a simple vision focused on improving the organization and ultimately winning. The leaders were persistent in communicating the vision and in winning "the right way." Even in high-pressure and challenging situations, the leaders were steadfast and did not compromise their vision or values.[1]

STAFF BUILDING

My first hire was Yinon Rietti, an international professional men's coach in Israel who was a long-time friend and had been my assistant briefly at Windsor while completing his master's degree. Yinon is an excellent player development coach. He has experience dealing with and training professional and Olympic athletes. I knew he would get respect from the players and be able to work them out daily at improving their skills. Connected in the European market, he would be my right hand to help with player identification, evaluation, and procurement. Lastly, I knew he would be an asset as a coach helping with strategies and systems.

My next hire was Will Rooney, who had connections with the Raptors 905, the NBA G League affiliate of the Toronto Raptors, as a volunteer manager. While he was only 25 years old with no previous direct experience in coaching, I had the immediate impression that he was a "grinder," the type who would do anything for the franchise because he wanted to move up in the ranks. I had previously met Will at my first Raptors 905 practice; we were the only two sitting in the team room waiting for a video session. We had introduced ourselves, and I had been impressed to learn his vision: to become an NBA coach. Under our overarching Honey Badgers vision to develop young professionals, I was in a position where I could help him get his first-ever coaching gig. Hiring Will was a great decision as he proved to be the very hard worker I had expected, learning to coach, giving spot-on advice in games, taking stats, and never saying no to anything we asked him to do. Will grew exponentially as a professional coach that summer.

My next hire was Kenold Knight, a local Hamiltonian coach and a full-time assistant for the local university men's basketball team. We met in the lobby of the Sheraton hotel in downtown Hamilton to discuss the opportunity. Though I appreciated his connection to the NBA—he was Shai Gilgeous-Alexander's mentor and personal coach at the time—what really struck me about Kenold were his values and outlook on life. He was a man of faith, a youth pastor, who specifically wanted to help young Black men to find their purpose. Kenold was an extremely qualified basketball coach who helped with scouting opponents (that was his job at McMaster), as well as helping with player character development—something John and I had talked about as a main goal of the franchise.

While working at developing all four pillars of the plan simultaneously, I was continuing to get ready for draft day, building a greater database of players. Building a professional sports franchise from the ground up would be enough to warrant an entire book, so here I will focus on the roster building process only: from pre-season all the way to the ascent.

> # TIME-OUT
> Research found that loyalty, trustworthiness, and strong personal values were deemed important by head coaches in choosing their assistant coaches. Additionally, the head coaches looked for assistant coaches who had a strong knowledge base that complemented their own skills and knowledge.[2]

ROSTER BUILDING

While building our roster, I turned to my long-time analytics consultant with the Windsor Lancers, Lucas Reindler, to help me crunch the statistics for every Canadian college and international player that was at our disposal from both the NCAA and U Sports to all the top Canadians playing abroad, as well as the entire NBA G League. Since the CEBL rosters had to have 70 percent Canadian players on each team, we needed to know who the best Canadian men were and get in touch with literally every available one. Beyond that, we also had to make sure that we identified the right three non-Canadian players on our roster. Focusing mainly on American players from the G League to find potential candidates, we created numerous lists of hundreds of names over a comprehensive 12-sheet Excel document that encompassed every Canadian male pro player, as well as NCAA and U Sports players, their contacts, and complete basketball statistics. We also included all the G League players, regardless of their nationalities.

This matrix was a big giant mess at the beginning; I did not know any of these players. I scouted by watching lots of video of these players on YouTube and Synergy (a basketball-specific video editing software available for coaches) to determine if I liked their game or not. I would then rank them in groups A, B, or C. Once we had our group A, I worked incredibly hard to research and contact players, which proved increasingly difficult. I was competing against the league's other GMs for the same players, and most of them had contacted players before I had even found their phone numbers, which was nothing short of an impossible task. That was when I shifted my focus to social media. I spent weeks systematically going through the hundreds of players on my spreadsheet and finding them on Instagram, Twitter, or Facebook and reaching them through private message channels. Yes, I DMed players through their social media accounts to get their cellphone numbers, which at the time was not a common practice at all. But like I said, it was the wild west and I had to get into the game.

Once I was able to get in touch with players, I created a simple system to record whether they were respectful on the phone, interested, available to join the team in the right time period for the season, what position they would fill on the depth chart, and their salary expectation. Slowly but surely, I began to enjoy the interaction with the players and started to build relationships with their agents. In an Excel document, I mapped all the players still to be reached, players interested, players willing to commit but in salary negotiation, players committed to be drafted by us, and players not interested or already committed elsewhere. The league had been clear that should we draft a player, we needed a letter of intent signed by him and his agent stipulating that he would be willing to play for the Honey Badgers should we select him.

Another critical point to our player evaluation was the emphasis both John and I put on finding good men, great citizens, and people of exemplary character. While it was easier to start identifying the players from a talent perspective, we then began to rank character over talent, since high performers often have an abundance of both traits. At that level of equal talent, my main focus was to equip myself with players I could trust, and who I felt would buy into my leadership as a coach. I built a small evaluation tool based on non-negotiables that we looked for in these men: Would they respond promptly to text messages, look me in the eye when I spoke, have a clean record of behaviour on and off the basketball court? Were they involved in their communities? Were they team captains? Were they trustworthy in taking care of their bodies (no drug or alcohol abuse)? Those behaviours were as important as their talent because the last thing we wanted were troublemakers or high-maintenance people. We did pass on a few very talented players, some who even had NBA experience, because of character.

> ## TIME-OUT
> Studies have found that athlete coachability (or character) has been identified as a critical component by elite level coaches in its effect on athlete performance success. Coachability refers to athletes sharing information with the coach, the level of trust and respect displayed towards the coach, flexibility and adaptability in changing routines, and an athlete's enthusiasm for seeking feedback and information from other resources.[3]

Preparing a draft list, and ultimately a working roster, I had so many moving pieces to keep in mind. I had to build the team of top players, yes, but I also had to manage the salary caps, players' availability based on contracts and schedules with pro leagues in Europe and Asia, as well as work around some of the best players looking to participate in the NBA Summer League in July, which overlapped with a quarter of our season. This was particularly difficult because every player's agent represented that their player would be playing in the NBA Summer League, though ultimately very few did. Who was I to say if they were good enough to play at that level or not? We opted to agree to get a bigger pool of interested players so we could deal with players arriving late, finishing playoffs with other teams, leaving midway to join the NBA Summer League, or leaving early to start their training camp in Europe. If a player was good enough and of good character, we would deal with his schedule after acquiring his rights.

DRAFT DAY

Prior to the CEBL, I had never been a part of a player draft of any kind. I didn't really have a clear concept of what a war room was. I didn't know what a draft table was or even how a snake draft operated. On my way home from Australia on the plane, I watched the movie *Draft Day* with Kevin Costner to try to get a bit of an idea of what I was getting myself into. I remember thinking that his character's life was just like mine: always on the phone making deals, negotiating, losing a player, gaining another one, not sleeping much, and not having any other life but his team! It's somewhat embarrassing to say, but the movie helped me understand and prepare for how the draft day would work. That is how little I knew about being a GM.

On our draft day, I was on and off the phone with numerous players that I had been in touch with who remained on our draft board. I remember getting a phone call from Duane Notice and MiKyle McIntosh, two of the top players from the Raptors 905 whom we wanted to be our top two draft picks. We knew that it would be important to get NBA-level talent with experience in the G League, so to get their commitment to sign only with us shortly before the draft was such a high. My mother was in town visiting at the time, and I remember hanging up and running to give her a big hug, saying, "I am going to nail this draft!" I prepared to join John and Lucas at the Best Western Plus Waterfront Hotel in Windsor, site of the Honey Badgers war room. When I got to the room, John informed me that another team had contacted our draft-committed G League players. I called that GM and told him to keep his distance from our players. When I asked John if my phone call had been okay, he looked at me wide-eyed and said, "I am sure you just scared the shit out of him!"

The thrill of drafting and being on the clock was incredible. All the scouting, evaluating skills and character, building rapport, and contract negotiating culminated in declaring on the spot, with a three-minute clock running down, the name to be drafted. It was a competitive thrill in and of itself, and it was surprising to see which players each GM had carefully chosen and when in the draft rounds they picked those players. Hamilton owned the fifth pick in the first round of the 2019 CEBL Entry Draft. We had targeted three Raptors 905 players, and for the first pick in franchise history, we selected forward MiKyle McIntosh, a Torontonian who had played at the University of Oregon, our team president's alma mater and where he had begun his professional career. We later selected McIntosh's Raptors 905 teammate, Duane Notice, followed by Derek Cooke Jr., Justin Edwards, Murphy Burnatowski, Tramar Sutherland, Joe Rocca, Erik Nissen, Ryan Ejim, Shaquille Keith, and Junior Cadougan. Finally, Thomas Kennedy and Connor Gilmore were the two Canadian university players we selected that day in the two-round U Sports draft that followed the entry draft.

In each case, I had developed great rapport with the player for multiple weeks prior to the draft by staying in touch over phone and text. I would watch their games and stats and send congrats or feedback. I would send some of the systems I was thinking of implementing with the team, letting them know how I saw them fit into the team. I would ask them what they thought of other players I was considering.

Coaching these men was going to be a new experience for me. It was professional basketball, and I was going to be measured on wins and losses and if I could craft a championship team, not on how nice or considerate I was with my staff or their opinions of me. I wanted to draft men I had already had direct contact and discussions with for these reasons. John and Lucas were not impressed with a player who in my opinion would be our starting point guard, the position I had spent the most time working on. A point guard is the extension of the coach, and I had had many great discussions with this player over the months preceding the draft. I knew he would fit my system and personality well, but they wanted someone else. When our time on the clock came around to draft in the sixth round, both John and Lucas respectfully remained quiet and let me make my own choice. I felt *bad*. We were a team, after all. I had to trust them and not be that stubborn—right? I made the decision in a split second as I heard myself say the name of their preference, not the point guard that I wanted. I immediately felt a knot in my stomach even though my words were met with looks of approval in the room. In the heat of the moment, I had decided to rely on the opinion of others in our organization over the word I had given this other athlete, and over my sense of intuition that he would be the best choice. I would now have to explain to him that a different decision was made, and I had no legitimate explanation other than the truth. I did not have the courage to stick to my guns. That moment tarnished my day. However, we still had a great draft on paper, probably the best draft of all the teams.

The young man I had promised to draft signed with a different team and became exactly what I had envisioned him to be: an excellent leader, floor general, and starting point guard. John later humbly admitted, "Chantal, you were right about that point guard. He had the season you said he would have, and he's a heckuva player for this league." This taught me the good lesson to stay true to my values, especially when the decision is difficult. Not that I didn't already know that, right?

> # TIME-OUT
> A case study on Bill Belichick demonstrated how he became the leader of the most successful professional sports franchise in North America in the 2000s. It is widely known that Belichick had final say on all personnel decisions. He saw value in players where other teams did not, moving on from key players at the right time, and always operating with the long view in mind. Belichick's forward-thinking innovative approach seemingly always had the New England Patriots one step ahead of the competition.[4]

While league observers had already been active on social media, giving the highest marks to our draft, there was no time to pat ourselves on the back. I was already working the phone to speak with undrafted players from our prospects lists to gauge their interest in signing a free agent contract or coming to training camp. We knew some of the players we had drafted would not be able to join our team until mid-season. There was much work to do before the full framework of our roster could take shape. I was learning that a GM's job is never done. In fact, the workload ramped up even further. I always kept in the back of my mind that as the first woman to serve as both a GM and head coach of a men's professional team, how I fared could impact future opportunities for other women. That was an added layer of pressure.

THE SEASON

Between the draft in March and the season opener in May, the workload and necessary preparation tripled. Now we had a roster, but it became a logistical nightmare because some players were still active on teams deep into playoffs and could not be present at training camp. Others had been injured or needed a two-week break before starting a new season. Our coaching staff assembled for the first time just a week before the start of training camp. We rented an Airbnb and together planned our systems, determined our roles, and even created a detailed schedule to give the players so they would understand the parameters we wanted to work within.

At the first practice, meeting the entire team, I was definitely nervous, but I knew as soon as the ball began to bounce that I would feel right at home. And I did. We implemented our systems, trained the men, and worked at scouting our first opponent. On May 12, 2019, at our home season opener, I got my first pro win with a 103–86 victory over Edmonton. The guys signed the game ball for me as I was greeted with cheers in the team room. We continued to win as a team and made our way to a respectable 7–3 start, tied for first in our division. Everyone was happy. I was looking forward to winning more games and continuing to grow as a team. I'll always remember when one of our players was interviewed and asked how he liked playing for me, and he glowingly responded that he loved playing for a woman coach! I could not have asked for a better experience in my first half of the season. I was ecstatic.

As it goes with any season, and as we have learned in the Third Quarter of this book, the grind eventually and inevitably sets in. First, the difficult travelling schedule across the country was getting to us. Second, most of us had moved into the local college residence, and the routine on long hot summer days was starting to feel cumbersome. On our longest plane trip of the season, a 6 p.m. flight got delayed to 11 p.m. We had arrived at the airport in the afternoon but did not leave until after midnight. After a six-hour flight, we arrived as the sun was coming up. We played that same night and were back on the plane for another red-eye. Upon our return home, we met the next day for a morning shoot-around and had another game that night. It was gruelling. We travelled coach on low-economy airlines always packed with people and with no extra room for anyone. Even at five-foot-eight, I felt a six-hour flight was difficult on my legs. I could not imagine how any of my six-foot to six-foot-eleven players could handle it.

At this point in the season, professional players had already competed for eight months with their overseas pro clubs, and the rigours of our arduous travel schedule was more than what several cared to endure in the summertime. One of our key starters, and likely one of our most talented players, decided he'd had enough after that particular trip. He simply never returned. I later received a text from him saying he appreciated his time and had nothing but positive things to say, but that it was just too much after a long regular season to commit to the amount of travel that was expected in our league.

No later than a week after this, another starter was told by his NBA club that he would be invited to their NBA Summer League team in Las Vegas, only to have that opportunity later withdrawn. As a result, he completely lost focus and interest in all things related to basketball and life. He and his best friend on the team were constantly distracted, which bothered the rest of the players, and our practices became a drag. We had to constantly get them to stop fooling around and to work harder. It was a pain. In the end, as the GM, I fined them more than I ever expected to, and tensions started to rise. Another player who had had enough of the two men's attitudes decided to quit the team.

TIME-OUT

As research demonstrates, the pressure and expectation to mould a group of professional athletes into a cohesive unit that produces rapid on-field success becomes a significant coaching challenge: "[difficult] athletes end up taking a lot of management time. If 80% of the time is spent with the negative players, not enough time is spent on reinforcing positive or good behaviours."[5] This implies that the presence of a difficult team member—who withholds effort, expresses negative emotions, breaks team rules, and/or mistreats teammates—negatively affects the team in terms of cohesion, satisfaction, and performance, and that team member's behaviour inhibits the coach's ability to effectively fulfill their role.[6]

I debated whether I should cut these two many times, but I never did because they would always show signs of commitment, respect, or a great game just at the right time to save themselves. It was also now the middle of the summer, and it would have been very difficult to replace their talent. I went against my own values and kept talent over low-maintenance behaviour and regretted this too. It was not that these men did not have good character, because they did, but at that time, with what was happening in their lives, they were distracted and distracting.

More distractions occurred than we had expected in a league that operated only from May through August. Because it was their typical off-season, players would randomly step away from the team to attend a family gathering or a wedding, and we had to call in replacement players from time to time to adjust. Our 7–3 team evolved into a club that went 3–7 for the second half of the season, playing against the same five other opponents. We were all collectively miserable. And before I knew it, I was as well. I began to wonder, "What happened to us?"

I knew I had to make drastic changes. Removing players and transforming the roster mid-season as a GM created some mistrust of me, as a coach, among the players who remained. When it was all said and done, we replaced two of five starters, and five of ten overall on the roster, with less than ten games left in the season. It was most difficult for the players who remained. Ironically, they remained on the roster because of their professionalism and commitment to excellence, but the roster changes had created a sense of unease and fear. Not the culture or collaboration I was looking for. It seemed like we were a sinking ship.

It had always been emphasized to me that in the end this was a pro team, and the players were all professionals from other leagues and therefore putting together a team that could make the playoffs and then win it all in August was the ultimate goal. A stellar regular season record was meaningless unless a team could win in the playoffs. For the franchise, the struggles of an inaugural regular season would quickly be forgotten with a championship win and heads held high in August. I worked tirelessly towards this goal by retooling our roster late in the regular season with an eye on winning the game that mattered most: the CEBL championship.

While some players stepped out, others stepped up, especially our veterans, who had the discipline and maturity that some younger players lacked. Because of the changes to the team, I had amassed enough salary cap room to make attractive offers to players who I knew could propel us to win the championship. I was constantly on calls with their agents, dealing as best I could to get the players I wanted. First, we added Keanau Post, a mature professional with Canadian national team and NBA G League experience when we had about eight games to go. Then we convinced two other great NBA G League players to finally fulfill their contract with six games to go, Duane Notice and MiKyle McIntosh. Then, with only four games left in the regular season and just before the league deadline to sign free agents, we signed Canadian scoring machine Xavier Rathan-Mayes, who had extensive NBA G League experience and a stint with the NBA's Memphis Grizzlies. Xavier is probably the most talented player I coached. With his scoring and playmaking ability, he was a player who could almost single-handedly win the final games for our team in August.

I had gotten to know these guys during the roster and draft building process, and I knew that they would not commit to an entire season. However, the added incentive of a bonus upon signing helped us win them over. I used the same strategy that NBA teams use when they know they have a team that can win the championship but need to fine-tune their roster and increase the quality and talent of their team: they go get what is missing to construct a roster that can win a championship.

ASCENDING

The season of ups and downs finished with a mid-pack record of ten wins and ten losses, which was good enough for fourth overall in the six-team league. Lots of turmoil had been endured, but I was hopeful that the team would be ready for the playoffs. The players all knew no more changes were coming, and I was hoping everyone could now pull together and focus on the playoffs. Like a sprinter on a track, I felt we had to just push through and dig deep for one more big finish.

I was confident in the roster, but the shuffle did not draw the culture that I had hoped for. Our new point guard with NBA experience had gotten into a verbal confrontation with some of the teammates at practice. A team veteran that I connected well with and had named captain was challenged daily by this new point guard. With the changes, the younger members of the team deferred to the NBA point guard as the alpha dog, as opposed to our veteran, who was always on the same page with me. The first practice we had for championship weekend was a disaster. Guys were yelling at each other, and none of us coaches could control it effectively to accomplish what we needed during that practice. The new point guard and our captain were in a dogfight for two days. I ended up letting the team scrimmage, hoping they would figure it out among themselves, but that didn't happen.

The afternoon before the championship semi-final, I decided to take our point guard for a walk, just to get to know him a bit better and let him air any gripes he might have. I also needed to pass the message that he was taking too many shots and not creating enough for his teammates, We needed less scoring and more assists from him. I decided to start by asking general questions about his family and ambitions and about his NBA experience. In the end, we sat down on a bench at a public park across from the hotel, and I told him, "Look, we need you to win tomorrow, and we need you to lead the team and rally the guys behind you. You are an excellent scorer, world class at that! For us to win tomorrow, we need a little bit more assists and a little less shot attempts . . ." I was carefully choosing my words.

He knew I was trying to address the commotion of the last two practices, but for whatever reason, he got very emotional and started shouting straight at my face, complaining about the league, the team, and my coaching credentials. I was stunned. I had had young women yell at me before because they were angry or frustrated, but they were 20-year-old student-athletes. More often than not, they had a lot of other things going on in their lives and were looking for someone to blame for their hardships. Here, I had a grown man who played in the NBA, six-foot-four, 220 pounds, with tattoos, yelling two inches from my face. And then it came: he began ranting how I had only coached "women" and didn't know how to coach "pros." It was an adult tantrum that lasted for several minutes. It was so loud it alerted people in the park, who looked over to see if I needed help. It felt awful, to say the least. I purposely held my ground, close to his face, so I would not let myself be intimidated. In that moment, all I could think about was to hold strong, not move, show no fear, and to just take it. I looked him straight in the eyes during the entire monologue of abusive language he hurled my way. I pulled my head and my chest up, braced my core as if to protect myself as though I was getting punched, and listened to him without blinking.

Then it stopped, as abruptly as it began. I took deep breath and said (as though I didn't have a care in the world), "Are you done?" He looked at me puzzled and kind of nodded. I then added calmly and firmly, perhaps with some colourful language thrown in, still not having lost eye contact, "Maybe you do not respect me as a coach, and maybe you think women's basketball is shit. Maybe you do not trust me as a GM. Maybe you think I'm overwhelmed or out of place. But I am going to tell you one thing you will respect about me: you will respect that I just stood here and took your yelling like a grown-ass adult. You will respect how I looked you straight in the eyes and just took all this shit. Maybe you don't respect me, but you will respect that."

I paused for a short moment and then I went on to do the only thing that my decades of leadership trained me to do: I laid down the vision and the game plan for him. I told him that if he thought he knew better than me and the rest of the guys, then it was time to show it. I told him that I'd give him the opportunity to lead the team tomorrow, even over our current team captain. But I gave him one challenge: to beat the number one ranked team the next day and prove that he was, in fact, the best. I told him he could only achieve that by showing up, performing, and rallying the entire team behind him. This meant respecting the team captain, passing the ball and involving his entire team, and letting me coach the way I coach and make the decisions that need to be made. After that, we talked a bit longer, but frankly I don't remember much else of what happened from then on. He had come at me. He challenged me as a coach, as a person, as a woman, and I stood my ground, and I took it. And in that moment, I transformed that relationship into the best collaboration I could, given the situation. It wasn't fixed, we weren't best friends, but we were business partners and collaborators, and what was said was said. Now we had a job to do.

TIME-OUT

Research states that in professional sports, there is a win-at-all-costs attitude.[7] Many professional coaches lose their jobs at the end of the competitive season if their team did not live up to the expectations on the field of play.[8]

We walked back to the hotel without talking. We sat down, and he showed me a bunch of plays he wanted to run and what defence he wanted to use. He wanted to be heard. The odd thing was that almost all of his ideas and strategies were exactly what we had already been doing. Had he not been paying attention? I played along and agreed with him on his feedback and on what he thought we should do, but I realized it was a very easy fix for me to let him believe I made changes to our plan. I'll also say that he did add two key points to the game plan that were great ideas, and I willingly adopted them and put them in.

The next day, I went to the shoot-around practice before the game and showed the guys what the game plan was, which had two little adjustments, and then let our point guard meet with the team. Since not much had changed, it was easy for everyone to follow a well-run practice. I let the point guard lead some of the drills, and for a short while, it seemed that we worked well together.

A few hours later, we were in the middle of the semi-final game, which was one of the most intense and difficult games I have ever coached. Still, I was focused. I took great time-outs. The team was united. Our point guard was stellar. In the very last seconds of the game, we were up one and the other team was at the free throw line. I took a time-out to try to ice the shooter, hoping that with the extra time on the bench he might freeze up mentally and miss his free throws. He did. We took the defensive rebound, and the buzzer rang.

In exhilarating chaos, we all jumped off the floor and hugged each other. I had never felt such a rush of energy fill my body or such relief take hold of my soul. Winning often brings more relief than joy. The players were so excited and proud; we seemed to be an unshakable unit. We made the league final in a major upset by beating the top-seed team. As I type this, I remember the happiness that enveloped me. It was like no other, as good and maybe better than winning a national championship. Why? Because even though I felt like I had been punched in the teeth by a player right before, I had had the knowledge, capacity, and emotional intelligence to respond the right way and lead the team through this adversity to a stunning victory.

No one knew what I had been through, but I knew. It was an incredible sense of self-achievement. I had just been yelled at by a former NBA player who clearly had little to no respect for me, but I found a way to garner enough of a bond to collaborate, plan, and rally him to play how he should. It was probably a display of my best leadership management ever, and I knew it.

A few minutes later, that point guard and I were headed down the arena corridor into the press room walking side by side for the post-game media conference. Upsetting the team that had won the regular season was a huge deal—the highlight of the season to that point. On our way there, I glanced at him and offered with a smile. "Yesterday it looked like we hated each other and today we are walking alongside like a head coach and her point guard who work well together, as it should be, both having just won and you having led the team to victory as the big dog with 28 points and 11 assists. Well done."

He just smiled.

The guys were so happy that night. We were headed to the championship final the next day. On Sunday, we had a walkthrough. We played a pretty good game as a team, but we looked tired. We had not played back-to-back games all season, and the elation of the win the day before had worn off, and the grind of the final set in. Our opponent, the host team for the championship event, was not more talented than the number one seed we'd dispelled the day before, but they were methodical in their plan and their defence. Our best three-point shooter went one for ten forcing shots because he barely touched the ball. Indeed, our point guard fell back into old habits, putting up 40 shots (40!), while ending with only one assist. We ended up losing a hard-fought game 94–83 in a contest that was closer than the final score would suggest. In that moment, tired and under the pressure of the final and of our own impressive showing the day before, our guys could not pull together as well as they had in the semi-final game. Our point guard took way too many shots and did not pass the ball. He had no interest in playing with his teammates. At one point, I wanted to substitute him out of the game, and he straight-up refused to come off. As much as the previous day had been a miracle of motivation and psychological leadership, the final was the complete opposite: a failure of culture. Nothing was going to keep the team, and this player, together this time. I was unable to lead him to play twice in a row in the way we needed for the team to win.

I now understand firsthand what NBA coaches mean when they talk about managing egos. Sometimes, egos take over and a team loses. Two of the players that I had traded or cut mid-season were picked up by the team we played in the finals, and they had a hell of a game. They played with a chip on their shoulders, and they were amazing. As classic as it can be, one of them, about six-foot-seven and 240 pounds, stared at me for the last minute of the game from the sideline just in front of where I was sitting. I thought, "Oh no! Another guy who is going to have an adult tantrum and give me an earful." I knew how upset he had been when we did not play him one game and when he had heard rumours of being traded. Then we had released him just before the deadline with little chance of getting picked up by a team. But here he was shooting me looks while winning the championship game. I looked at him for a moment and tried to calm the situation, but in the end, I ignored him through to the final buzzer. It was definitely poetic justice for him and his teammate whom we had let go.

Overall, I was disappointed but not devastated. Of course, I had not achieved my plan and the vision I had set out for myself. We came short by 11 points in the final. The Honey Badgers did not win a championship in year one. Although the end goal wasn't achieved, the process taught me something about myself and my coaching, about building culture and committing to goals, about fundamental truths and personal resilience. And that's why I consider my year an immense success. It was an experience I will cherish for the rest of my life.

REFLECTION

Should I ever coach the pros again, I would use a different model and vision. First, I would ensure I could commit to a multi-year plan that puts the emphasis on players and franchise development as a long-term investment in these men. I would not focus on or condone short-term winning. Even for the professional ranks, trusting the process, like Philadelphia 76ers general manager Sam Hinkie did, is still a better option than trying to fix everything quickly for the sake of winning in a one-year span. Players' trust and buy-in are crucial to the health of an organization. Additionally, when the same players and coaches return year after year, trust grows; working towards a long-term vision is then possible, and a desired culture is easier to achieve.

The hiring and firing of players throughout the summer was not conducive to optimal culture building; it also did not enable me to uphold the principle that I live by at the University of Windsor: "First relationships, then championships." Starting with draft day and throughout the entire season as the general manager, I was living with mixed messages. I justified many of my short-term choices by believing that a professional team was different. The pros can take it. In hindsight, I see how that it is not all that different. I still hold that winning is the by-product of investing in individuals. For this one summer, there was some of that, but there was more moving players around to get to the goal quick. With this experience under my belt, I developed an aversion to the fast-paced, ever-changing style that a GM can opt for in professional sports, particularly when players are treated as disposable assets for the franchise's benefit. Investing in the development of athletes first should be the priority.

When I started in the CEBL, I expected it would be very different to coach men versus women, but surprisingly it was not. An athlete is an athlete, and basketball reads and plays the same way, as I came to realize. I thoroughly enjoyed coaching men, and to be the only female coach in the league at the time was an honour and a great learning opportunity. Perhaps the story of the point guard yelling at me surprised you. Really, it caused me to wonder how many women are ready for this type of interaction in the men's professional world. Perhaps more broadly, no matter what the gender, intense high-competition sports generate difficult discussions and communication environments. I am thankful that I reacted in a way that brought a positive change to our team that summer, even if for one day. Managing grown men's egos and strong personalities is what I learned the most about and was my biggest learning curve to coaching the pros. It made me a better leader and a better coach. Yet I made mistakes and did not always take my own advice and knowledge to heart. I say this to let others who read this know that it doesn't always go as planned, but that the process of self-evaluation, growth, and striving towards mastery is never-ending, win, lose, or draw.

CHAPTER 17

Role of Women in Coaching

From the moment I was announced as the general manager and head coach of the Hamilton Honey Badgers and when, shortly after, it was decided that each GM would recruit and draft their own roster, I worked a minimum of 80 hours a week non-stop, from January until the end of the season in August. I was constantly feeling the pressure to win. Outside of the fact that I had never coached professional men, that I had never been a true GM, that the league was entirely new, and I had no history to draw from, there was the *additional* pressure I felt that none of the other coaches had to manage—the gender barrier, the asterisk beside my name as coach and general manager. "Oh, and by the way, she's a woman" might follow me, and other women coaches, if I didn't win the championship.

It made me think of all the women in sports who had to face doubters and naysayers. People's quiet comments in the hallways. It wasn't front and centre, but it was still there. I knew I had to prove myself *again*. There was no way that I could lose, because it would be bigger than just me if I did. If I failed, it would be labelled as the failure, the inability, of women to coach men, to be GMs and leaders in the executive offices of pro men's sports. I feared that it would set back women's efforts for equality in sports. It kept playing on repeat in my mind. I was sure that my success would open doors for more women in sports all over the world.

TIME-OUT

Research has found that female coaches often feel the pressure to constantly prove themselves in order to gain respect from male colleagues. These additional stressors in the workplace often lead to female coaches experiencing stress and burnout.[1]

The media played a role in adding pressure, but I welcomed it. I was keenly aware that my platform would give me the opportunity to provide guidance and inspiration to the next generation of young women. Media plays such an important role in the representation and coverage of women in sports. Much of what we grow up to believe, think, act, do, and emulate is shaped by television and people we see in the media. If the media continues to show only a very small percentage of women on TV or write minimally of women in sports in print or social media, the balance of opportunity, and enrichment of the sport, is not going to change. If people see the value of women on their television screens or their social media feeds, they will be more willing to see women in leadership positions, in positions of power elsewhere in our society, and this will translate much more broadly beyond the CEBL or basketball itself. Jean Williams, a professor in sport history and author of women's history, suggests that an entire doctrinal shift is necessary for changing society's viewpoint when it comes to comparing women and men in sports, which trickles down to unequal funding, media interest, and career opportunities.

One of the most notable female coaches in NCAA history is Muffet McGraw. She coached Notre Dame's basketball team for 32 years and is a huge advocate of women in sports. She is constantly pushing for more women role models, more visible women leaders, more women in power. She believes, as I do, that it is a scary fact that girls often grow up with traditional gender roles already set—that men run the world, have the power, and make the decisions. Ultimately, all of society suffers because of this bias. Young girls need someone to look up to and tell them that this is not the way it has to be. McGraw firmly believes there is no better way to do this than with sports. We need to teach young people how to watch the way women lead so we can get to a point where 50 percent of the people in power are women. "People hire people who look like them, and that's the problem," said McGraw. We need to change this and have higher equality of women in sports, and in all avenues of life.

> **TIME-OUT**
>
> There is emerging evidence in sport[2] and non-sport[3] contexts that developmental agents, such as mentors, can promote the advancement of women's careers by providing support to help navigate systemic barriers. Researchers suggest that sports psychology scholars should further examine the developmental impact of female role models, and the potential advantage of fostering vast and buried developmental networks for the advancement of women in sport.

There are quite a few women who have broken the gender barrier in sports in recent years. Andy Murray, a former number one tennis player in the world, went against the norm and hired a woman, Amelie Mauresmo, as his coach from 2014 to 2016. Becky Hammon has been an assistant coach in the NBA since 2014 and filled in as the head coach during a game after her head coach was ejected. Kim Ng became the first female general manager in major league baseball. The NFL also boasts eight women coaches and made history when six of them coached in the playoffs and two became the first women to win the Super Bowl as coaches. In 2021, referee Sarah Thomas became the first woman to officiate in a Super Bowl. Although these are amazing accomplishments for women, we still have a long way to go. But the possibilities are endless.

And what has become of women in the CEBL? Well, I'm extremely happy to say that there continues to be a positive progression of women in the league, and four women served as assistant coaches in its second year. More women have been hired as assistant coaches for the third season, and the league office hired a woman to serve as its director of Montreal operations as the league pursues its intention of adding an expansion team in Quebec. Women have half of the management positions within the CEBL office and fill key roles in each front office across the league.

TIME-OUT

Despite the advances towards empowering women in sport, research suggests that continued effort needs to be made to include men in these initiatives and educate them on gender-based barriers faced by women coaches and athletes. Bringing awareness to the barriers and challenges that women coaches face, and creating female role models in leadership positions, may help empower the next generation of girls towards achieving leadership positions in sport.[4]

It's my hope that everyone can use the steps and the stories I have shared in this book to enrich their self-knowledge, self-love, and self-growth. In the end, it's the only way to challenge yourself to be the best you that you possibly can be.

POST-GAME

We have gone through the game, including all four quarters, time-outs, and even an overtime. The four quarters have given us a structure, which, if followed, is sure to set any leader on the path towards success. The overtime has proven that using these tips and processes can help anyone build and transform a program effectively and quickly. To create a championship team, a vision needs to be clearly communicated and sold. Equally as important as the vision is the culture. Culture is at times action and at times transformation, but in the end, it is about driving a common and shareable belief system that produces results. It must provide happiness and enjoyment for those who are part of it. It is also important to note that the culture and vision of the team must adapt and change as both the team and society evolve.

For a leader of a group of people, opportunity doubles as a chance for introspection and growth. Leading a group of people is like entering the Simulator but in real-life. Going through the process of becoming a successful leader is an entirely different experience from studying it theoretically. There are many moments and opportunities to re-evaluate, recentre, and reinvent oneself. Mentors play a crucial role in guiding every successful leader's journey.

A leadership style that is both demanding and caring, loving and tough, transactional and transformational, gritty and flexible, will allow people to shine. Leaders also get an edge when they control their minds, which also allows them to model that skill for their team. In any competitive or performative realm, "going for the kill" calls for performers who can remain calm in the middle of chaos and allow their grittiness to take over when facing obstacles. Ever-changing experiences, teams, players, and generations will continue to bring about new challenges that demand coaches to remain steadfast in the pursuit of mastery.

Transforming the University of Windsor women's basketball team ultimately transformed me. Working with the pros during my sabbatical transformed me even further. The teams and players I have coached have shaped who I am and who I will be in the future. This is a lifelong process. I have taken all that I have learned even further by applying the principles of *Dare to Win* beyond coaching to my entire life. Whether the people who have been part of my journey have been coaches, players, parents, referees, therapists, or support staff, they have shaped who I am today, and I owed it to them to write about it.

NOTES

CHAPTER 1: UNLEASHING THE POWER OF VISION

1. Teresa L. Heiland, Robert Rovetti, and Jan Dunn, "Effects of visual, auditory, and kinesthetic imagery interventions on dancers' plié arabesques," *Journal of Imagery Research in Sport and Physical Activity* 7, no. 1 (2012), doi.org/10.1515/1932-0191.1065; Phillip G. Post, Craig A. Wrisberg, and Stephen Mullins, "A field test of the influence of pre-game imagery on basketball free throw shooting," *Journal of Imagery Research in Sport and Physical Activity* 5, no. 1 (2010), doi.org/10.2202 /1932-0191.1042; Nicolas Robin, Laurent Dominique, Lucette Toussaint, Yannick Blandin, Aymeric Guillot, and Michel Le Her, "Effects of motor imagery training on service return accuracy in tennis: The role of imagery ability," *International Journal of Sport and Exercise Psychology* 5, no. 2 (2007): 175–186, doi.org/10.1080/16121 97X.2007.9671818.
2. Caroline Wakefield and Dave Smith, "Perfecting practice: Applying the PETTLEP Model of motor imagery," *Journal of Sport Psychology in Action* 3, no. 1 (2012): 1–11, doi.org/10.1080/21520704.2011.639853.

CHAPTER 2: THE FIRST SEASON

1. William J. Heelis, Jeffrey G. Caron, and Gordon A. Bloom, "The experiences of high-performance coaches in the management of difficult athletes," *Psychology of Sport and Exercise* 51 (2020): 101751, doi.org/10.1016/j.psychsport.2020.101751. This study's key finding is based on interviews of eight coaches of junior hockey (ages 16–20) in Canada to better understand difficult athlete behaviours. More research on this topic is needed to provide guidance on this often misunderstood but important aspect of high-performance coaching (Leggat et al., 2020; Neely, Dunn, McHugh & Holt, 2016; Wachsmuth et al., 2018).

CHAPTER 3: CREATING A PLAN

1. David A. Urquhart, Gordon A. Bloom, and Todd Loughead, "The development, articulation, and implementation of a coaching vision of multiple championship-winning university ice hockey coaches," *International Sport Coaching Journal* 7, no. 3 (2020): 335–346, doi.org /10.1123/iscj.2019-0096. This article explores the crucial role that a coach's vision plays in creating and sustaining a culture of excellence. The researchers' sample was six men's university ice hockey head coaches who had a combined 20 national titles and over 4,100 wins.

CHAPTER 4: TRUSTING THE PROCESS

1. Outside sport psychology, research has begun to focus on the nature and effects of transformational leadership in organizations. A series of papers published by Bass and colleagues suggests that transformational leaders are, among other things, inspirational motivators who elevate the interest of their followers. Transformational leadership contains four leader behaviours that have been shown to influence followers' values, needs, awareness, and performance. See Bernard M. Bass, *Leadership and Performance*

Beyond Expectations (The Free Press, 1985); Bernard M. Bass, "Two decades of research and development in transformational leadership," *European Journal of Work and Organizational Psychology* 8, no. 1 (1999): 9–32, doi.org/10.1080/135943299398410; Bernard M. Bass and Bruce J. Avolio, *Improving Organizational Effectiveness Through Transformational Leadership* (Sage, 1993); and Bernard M. Bass and Ronald E. Riggio, *Transformational Leadership*, 2nd ed. (Lawrence Erlbaum, 2006).

2. Anita Elberse and Thomas Dye, "Sir Alex Ferguson: Managing Manchester United," Harvard Business School Case 513-051, September 2012. Sir Alex Ferguson's successful transformation of Manchester United demonstrates the impact that a high-performance leader can have on both the on-field performance and the monetary value of an organization.

3. Kyle Paradis, Albert V. Carron, and Luc J. Martin, "Athlete perceptions of intra-group conflict in sport teams," *Sport & Exercise Psychology Review* 10, no. 3 (2014): 4–18, doi.org/10.53841/bpssepr .2014.10.3.4. While the behaviours, actions, and attitudes of athletes may enhance the team environment and its cohesion, they may also deter it and lead to feelings of frustration and angst rather than fulfillment. See William J. Heelis, Jeffrey G. Caron, and Gordon A. Bloom, "The experiences of high-performance coaches in the management of difficult athletes," *Psychology of Sport and Exercise* 51 (2020): 101751, doi.org/10.1016/j.psychsport.2020.101751.

4. Nobert Kerr et al., "'How many bad apples does it take to spoil the whole barrel?': Social exclusion and toleration for bad apples," *Journal of Experimental Social Psychology* 45, no. 4 (2009): 603–613, doi.org/10.1016/j.jesp.2009.02.017.

5. M. J. Davies, Gordon A. Bloom, and J. H. Salmela, "Job satisfaction of accomplished male university basketball coaches: The Canadian context," *International Journal of Sport Psychology* 36, no. 3 (2005): 173–192. This study is based on interviews with six Canadian university head basketball coaches. Short and Short (2005) found that scholarship allotment and budget restrictions were other constraints that American head coaches dealt with on a regular basis.

CHAPTER 5: THE LIMITING FACTOR

1. Daniela Donoso-Morales, Gordon A. Bloom, and Jeffrey G. Caron, "Creating and sustaining a culture of excellence: Insights from accomplished university team-sport coaches," *Research Quarterly for Exercise and Sport* 88, no. 4 (2017): 503–512, doi.org/10.1080/027013 67.2017.1370531. Some of the coaches in this study also wrote notes for themselves about what they thought had negatively influenced the athletes' performance; these notes were used to improve team performance at subsequent tournaments.

2. Jennifer A. Villwock, Lindsay B. Sobin, Lindsey A. Koester, and Tucker M. Harris, "Imposter syndrome and burnout among American medical students: A pilot study," *International Journal of Medical Education* 7 (2016): 364–369, doi.org/10.5116/ijme.5801 .eac4. The researchers reported, "Assessments of students on a surgery rotation found that when asked to evaluate themselves, the female students gave themselves lower scores than the male students despite faculty evaluations that showed the women outperformed the men." A pattern in the research literature shows that women report experiencing imposter phenomenon more frequently than men, and that in particular women of colour are often afflicted with imposter syndrome in elite universities. The University of Michigan surveyed 400 students with a focus on imposter syndrome and noted that students do not readily identify IP but share feelings of inadequacy, low self-worth, and low self-confidence.

3. Valentina Perciavalle et al., "The role of deep breathing on stress," *Neurological Science* 38 (2017): 451–458, doi.org/10.1007/s10072-016-2790-8; Susan I. Hopper, Sherrie L. Murray, Lucille R. Ferrara, and Joanne K. Singleton, "Effectiveness of diaphragmatic breathing for reducing physiological and psychological stress in adults: A quantitative systemic review," *JBI Database of Systematic Reviews and Implementation Reports* 17, no. 9 (2019): 1855–1876, doi.org/10.11124 /JBISRIR-2017-003848.

CHAPTER 6: AN EMPIRE OF MENTORS

1. Jordan S. Lefebvre, Gordon A. Bloom, and Todd M. Loughead, "A citation network analysis of career mentoring across disciplines: A roadmap for mentoring research in sport," *Psychology of Sport and Exercise* 49 (2020): 101676, doi.org/10.1016/j.psychsport.2020.101676.

2. Judy McKimm, Carol Jollie, and Mark Hatter, "Mentoring: Theory and practice," *London NHSE* (2007). Available at faculty.londondeanery.ac.uk/e-learning/feedback/files/Mentoring_Theory_and_Practice.pdf/view.

3. John C. Kunich and Richard L. Lester, "Leadership and the art of mentoring: Tool kit for the time machine," *Journal of Leadership and Organizational Studies* 6, no. 1–2 (Winter/Spring 1999): 117–127, doi.org/10.1177/107179199900600102.

4. Jordan S. Lefebvre, Gordon A. Bloom, and Lindsay R. Duncan, "A qualitative examination of the developmental networks of elite sport coaches," *Sport, Exercise, and Performance Psychology* 10, no. 2 (2021): 310–326, doi.org/10.1037/spy0000254. This study interviewed nine experienced elite head coaches with an average of 21.44 years of head coaching experience at the university, professional, and/or national levels to learn who influenced their career progression. The findings indicated that coaches benefitted from relationships with other coaches, athletes, and family members that collectively contributed to their development on a personal and professional level. These results suggest that people learn and develop with assistance from multiple individuals, both inside and outside the sporting domain.

CHAPTER 8: TOP TEN LESSONS LEARNED FROM COACHING

1. Madison M. Fraser, Gordon A. Bloom, and Clifford J. Mallett, "University serial winning coaches' experiences with low performance and maladaptive team culture," *Psychology of Sport and Exercise* 74 (2024), doi.org/10.1016/j.psychsport.2024.102677; Zoe Knowles, David Gilbourne, Brendan Cropley, and Lindsey Dugdill, "Reflecting

on reflection and journeys," in *Reflective Practice in the Sport and Exercise Science: Contemporary Issues*, eds. Brendan Cropley and Zoe Knowles (Routledge, 2014); Zoe Knowles, David Gilbourne, Andy Borrie, and Alan Nevill, "Developing the reflective sports coach: A study exploring the processes of reflective practice within a higher education coaching programme," *Reflective Practice* 2, no. 2 (2001): 185–207, doi.org/10.1080/14623940123820.

CHAPTER 9: BUILDING CULTURE FOR THE GRIND

1. To learn more about the success of the New Zealand All Blacks, see Ken Hodge, Graham Henry, and Wayne Smith, "A case study of excellence in elite sport: Motivational climate in a world champion team," *The Sport Psychologist* 28, no. 1 (2014): 60–74, doi.org/10.1123 /tsp.2013-0037. Hodge and colleagues conducted a case study focusing on the team from 2004 to 2011. The purpose of this study was to examine the team's motivational climate and its impact on the All Blacks winning the 2011 Rugby World Cup. See also James Kerr, *Legacy: What the All Blacks Can Teach Us about the Business of Life* (Constable, 2013). Kerr spent five weeks with the All Blacks, studying the team culture as they prepared for the 2011 Rugby World Cup. Kerr wanted to understand why they were so successful. Results from both Hodge and colleagues and Kerr revealed that the secret to the All Blacks' unparalleled success is the team culture.

2. Gordon A. Bloom and Diane E. Stevens, "Case study: A team-building mental skills training program with an intercollegiate equestrian team," *Athletic Insight: The Online Journal of Sport Psychology* 4, no. 1 (2002), researchgate.net/publication/228988281_Case_study _A_team-building_mental_skills_training_program_with_an _intercollegiate_equestrian_team. This study investigated the use of a team-building intervention approach with a university equestrian team. The season-long intervention, based on information that the mental performance consultant acquired from the athletes and coaches pre-season, focused on leadership, team norms, communication, and competition issues.

3. Martin Camiré, Pierre Trudel, and Tanya Forneris, "Coaching and transferring life skills: Philosophies and strategies used by model high school coaches," *The Sport Psychologist* 26, no. 2 (2012): 243–260, doi.org /10.1123/tsp.26.2.243. This study, among others, suggests that youth sport participation is an avenue for fostering positive development and learning important life skills. These researches interviewed nine coaches and 16 of their student-athletes to examine the strategies used by high school coaches to teach and transfer life skills to non-sport settings. Athletes reported learning life skills such as communication, leadership, and teamwork and transferring them to non-sport settings. Life skills are defined as "internal personal assets, characteristics, and skills . . . that can be facilitated or developed in sport and are transferred for use in non-sport settings" in Daniel Gould and Sarah Carson, "Life skills development through sport: Current status and future directions," *International Review of Sport and Exercise Psychology* 1, no. 1 (2008): 58–78, doi.org/10.1080/17509840701834573. Youth sport participation was found to promote important life skills such as goal setting, time and stress management, emotional regulation, moral development, teamwork, and confidence in Daniel Gould, Sarah Carson, Angela Fifer, Larry Lauer, and Robert Benham, "Stakeholders' perceptions of social-emotional and life skill development issues characterizing contemporary high school sports," *Journal of Coaching Education* 2, no. 1 (2009): 20–44, doi.org/10.1123/jce.2.1.20.

4. K. Anders Ericsson, Ralf T. Krampe, and Clemens Tesch-Römer, "The role of deliberate practice in the acquisition of expert performance," *Psychological Review* 100, no. 3 (1993): 363–406, doi .org/10.1037/0033-295X.100.3.363.

CHAPTER 10: PLANNING FOR THE GRIND

1. Stephen M. Gavazzi, "Turning boys into men: The incentive-based system in Urban Meyer's plan to win," *International Sport Coaching Journal* 2, no. 3 (2015): 298–304, doi.org/10.1123/iscj.2015-0064.

2. Albert Bandura and Dale Schunk, "Cultivating competence, self-efficacy, and intrinsic interest through proximal self-motivation,"

Journal of Personality and Social Psychology 41, no. 3 (1981): 586–598, doi.org/10.1037/0022-3514.41.3.586.

CHAPTER 11: THE GLUE THAT HOLDS IT TOGETHER

1. William J. Heelis, Jeffrey G. Caron, and Gordon A. Bloom, "The experiences of high-performance coaches in the management of difficult athletes," *Psychology of Sport and Exercise* 51 (2020): 101751, doi.org/10.1016/j.psychsport.2020.101751. This study's key finding is based on interviews of eight coaches of junior hockey (ages 16–20) in Canada to better understand difficult athlete behaviours. More research on this topic is needed to provide guidance on this often misunderstood but important aspect of high-performance coaching (Leggat et al., 2020; Neely, Dunn, McHugh & Holt, 2016; Wachsmuth et al., 2018).

2. Inge Milius, Wade Gilbert, Danielle Alexander, and Gordon A. Bloom, "Coaches' use of positive tactile communication in collegiate basketball," *International Sport Coaching Journal* 8, no. 1 (2020): 91–100, doi.org/10.1123/iscj.2020-0001. These researchers studied members of a successful NCAA collegiate women's basketball team: the head coach, associate head coach, and 16 student-athletes.

CHAPTER 12: GRITTY TEAMS WIN

1. David Fletcher and Mustafa Sarkar, "Mental fortitude training: An evidence-based approach to developing psychological resilience for sustained success," *Journal of Sport Psychology in Action* 7, no. 3 (2016): 135–157, doi.org/10.1080/21520704.2016.1255496.

CHAPTER 13: GRIT-BOOSTING TECHNIQUES

1. Philippa Velija, Mark Mierzwinski, and Laura Fortune, "'It made me feel powerful': Women's gendered embodiment and physical empowerment in the martial arts," *Leisure Studies* 32, no. 5 (2013):

524–541, doi.org/10.1080/02614367.2012.696128. Velija and colleagues explored the physical empowerment and gendered embodiment of 11 women training in martial arts. They found that the participants developed a sense of physical (e.g., strength, power) and mental (e.g., confidence, perseverance) empowerment from participation in sport. Similar findings were documented by Toni Liechty, Fleesha Willfong, and Katie Sveinson, "Embodied experiences of empowerment among female tackle football players," *Sociology of Sport Journal* 33, no. 4 (2016): 305–316, doi.org/10.1123/ssj.2015-0149. Liechty and colleagues interviewed 15 women football players about their perceptions of embodied empowerment in sport. The athletes discussed sport as a means of providing physical strength, confidence, acceptance, and the opportunity to resist societal stereotypes concerning gender and sport. See also Candace Ashton-Shaeffer, Heather Gibson, Marieke Holt, and Cynthia Willming, "Women's resistance and empowerment through wheelchair sport," *World Leisure Journal* 43, no. 4 (2001): 11–21, doi.org/10.1080/04419057.2001.9674245. Ashton-Shaeffer and colleagues interviewed ten women wheelchair basketball players, and participants described sport as a means of gaining control over one's body and resisting the oppression and social stigma associated with disability. Sport was used as a means of empowerment on an individual level by enhancing self-perception, self-confidence, and sense of accomplishment, as well as on a collective level by developing a sense of responsibility to empower others.

2. Chris Beaumont, Ian W. Maynard, and Joanne Butt, "Effective ways to develop and maintain robust sport-confidence: Strategies advocated by sport psychology consultants," *Journal of Applied Sport Psychology* 27, no. 3 (2015): 301–318, doi.org/10.1080/104132 00.2014.996302; Kate Hays, Owen Thomas, Ian Maynard, and Mark Bawden, "The role of confidence in world-class sport performance," *Journal of Sports Sciences* 27, no. 11 (2009): 1185–1199, doi.org/10.1080/02640410903089798; Moe Machida, Mark Otten, T. Michelle Magyar, Robin S. Vealey, and Rose Marie Ward, "Examining multidimensional sport-confidence in athletes and non-athlete sport performers," *Journal of Sports Sciences* 35, no. 5 (2017): 410–418, doi.org/10.1080/02640414.2016.1167934.

3. George P. Hollenbeck and Douglas T. Hall, "Self-confidence and leader performance," *Organizational Dynamics* 33, no. 3 (2004): 254–269, doi.org/10.1016/j.orgdyn.2004.06.003.

4. Kate Hays, Ian Maynard, Owen Thomas, and Mark Bawden, "Sources and types of confidence identified by world class sport performers," *Journal of Applied Sport Psychology* 19, no. 4 (2007): 434–456, doi.org/10.1080/10413200701599173. This study identifies nine sources of confidence: "preparation, performance accomplishments, coaching, innate factors, social support, experience, competitive advantage, self-awareness, and trust."

5. Pedro Mateos-Aparicio and Antonio Rodríguez-Moreno, "The impact of the study of brain plasticity," *Frontiers in Cellular Neuroscience* 13 (2019): 66, doi.org/10.3389/fncel.2019.00066.

6. Sergio Lara-Bercial and Cliff Mallett, "The practices and developmental pathways of professional and Olympic serial winning coaches," *International Sport Coaching Journal* 3, no. 3 (2016): 221–239, doi.org/10.1123/iscj.2016-0083. This study showed that driven benevolence helped coaches build a serial winning program by simplifying complex ideas, having a strong sense of purpose, being able to manage pressures, and guarding against complacency. Additionally, these serial winning coaches were genuine, acted ethically, had high levels of emotional intelligence, and viewed their players as people first and athletes second. Understanding the components of the serial winning coach and the key principle of driven benevolence provides valuable insight into how high-performance sport leaders maximize their followers' potential in pursuit of building championship teams.

CHAPTER 14: STRIVING FOR MASTERY

1. Phil Jackson and Hugh Delehanty, *Sacred Hoops: Spiritual Lessons of a Hardwood Warrior* (Hyperion, 1995).

2. Sophia Jowett, "Interdependence analysis and the 3+1Cs in the coach-athlete relationship," in *Social Psychology in Sport*, eds. Sophia Jowett and David Lavallee (Human Kinetics, 2007), 15–27.

3. John Wooden, *They Call Me Coach* (Contemporary Books, 1988), 62.

4. Wooden, *They Call Me Coach*, 89.

CHAPTER 15: GOING PRO

1. Ivan Oterino, "Great GMs are made, not born," Korn Ferry, kornferry.com/insights/this-week-in-leadership/great-gms-are -made-not-born.
2. John P. Kotter and James L. Heskett, *Corporate Culture and Performance* (Simon and Schuster, 2008).

CHAPTER 16: THE PROCESS

1. Joe Frontiera, "Leadership and organizational culture transformation in professional sport," *Journal of Leadership & Organizational Studies* 17, no. 1 (2010): 71–86, doi.org/10.1177 /154805180934525.
2. Scott Rathwell, Gordon A. Bloom, and Todd Loughead, "Head coaches' perceptions on the roles, selection and development of the assistant coach," *International Sport Coaching Journal* 1, no. 1 (2014): 5–16, doi.org/10.1123/iscj.2013-0008.
3. Peter R. Giacobbi, Joe Whitney, Emily Roper, and Ted Butryn, "College coaches' views about the development of successful athletes: A descriptive exploratory investigation," *Journal of Sport Behavior* 25, no. 2 (2002): 17–28; Daniel Gould, Kristen Dieffenbach, and Aaron Moffett, "Psychological characteristics and their development in Olympic champions," *Journal of Applied Sport Psychology* 14, no. 3 (2002): 172–204, doi.org/10.1080/1041320029010 3482.
4. Michael Holley, *War Room: The Legacy of Bill Belichick and the Art of Building the Perfect Team* (HarperCollins, 2011).
5. Peter Olusoga, Joanne Butt, Kate Hays, and Ian Maynard, "Stress in elite coaching: Identifying stressors," *Journal of Applied Sport Psychology* 21, no. 4 (2009): 442–459, doi.org/10.1080/10413200903 222921.

6. Cassandra Cope, Mark A. Eys, Robert J. Schinke, and Grégoire Bosselut, "Coaches' perspectives of a negative informal role: The 'cancer' within sport teams," *Journal of Applied Sport Psychology* 22, no. 4 (2010): 420–436, doi.org/10.1080/10413200.2010.495327. When to cut a player from a team is one of the least understood aspects of coaching psychology. More research on this topic is needed.

7. Andrew Bennie and Donna O'Connor, "Coaching philosophies: Perceptions from professional cricket, Rugby League and Rugby Union players and coaches in Australia," *International Journal of Sports Science & Coaching* 5, no. 2 (2010), 309–320, doi.org/10.1260/1747-9541.5.2 .309; Peter Olusoga, Joanne Butt, Kate Hays and Ian Maynard, "Stress in elite sports coaching: Identifying stressors." *Journal of Applied Sport Psychology* 21, no. 4 (2009): 442–459, doi.org/10.1080/10413200903222921.

8. Cliff Mallett and Sergio Lara-Bercial, "Serial winning coaches: People, vision, and environment," in *Sport and Exercise Psychology Research: From Theory to Practice*, eds. Markus Raab, Paul Wylleman, Roland Seiler, Anne-Marie Elbe, and Antonis Hatzigeorgiadis (Elsevier, 2016), 289–322.

CHAPTER 17: ROLE OF WOMEN IN COACHING

1. Diane Culver, Erin Kraft, Cari Din, and Isabelle Cayer, "The Alberta women in sport leadership project: A social learning intervention for gender equity and leadership development," *Women in Sport and Physical Activity Journal* 27, no. 2 (2019): 110–117, doi.org /10.1123/wspaj.2018-0059; Nicole LaVoi and Julia K. Dutove, "Barriers and supports for female coaches: An ecological model," *Sports Coaching Review* 1, no. 1 (2012): 17–37, doi.org/10.1080/2164062 9.2012.695891.

2. Jenessa Banwell, Gretchen Kerr, and Ashley Stirling, "Benefits of a female coach mentorship programme on women coaches' development: An ecological perspective," *Sports Coaching Review* 10, no. 1 (2021): 61–83, doi.org/10.1080/21640629.2020.1764266; Jenessa Banwell, Gretchen Kerr, Ashley Stirling, "Key considerations for advancing women in coaching," *Women in Sport and Physical Activity*

Journal 27, no. 2 (2019): 128–135, doi.org/10.1123/wspaj
.2018-0069.

3. Jihyun Chang, Pyounggu Baek, and Taesung Kim, "Women's developmental networks and career satisfaction: Developmental functions as a mediator," *Journal of Career Development* 48, no. 5 (2021): 733–750, doi.org/10.1177/0894845319900005.

4. Danielle Alexander, Gordon A. Bloom, and Shaunna L. Taylor, "Female Paralympic athlete views on effective and ineffective coaching practices," *Journal of Applied Sport Psychology* 32, no. 1 (2020): 48–63, doi.org/10.1080/10413200.2018.1543735; Banwell, Kerr, and Stirling, "Benefits of a female coach mentorship programme."

BIBLIOGRAPHY

Q1

Adie, James W., and Sophia Jowett (2010). Meta-perceptions of the coach-athlete relationship, achievement goals, and intrinsic motivation among sport participants. *Journal of Applied Social Psychology*.

Associated Press (2011, July 19). Japan lifts weary nation's spirits. ESPN. http://www.espn.com/sports/soccer/news/_/id/6783054/2011-women -world-cup-victorious-japan-returns-heroes.

Avolio, Bruce J., and Bernard M. Bass (1991). *The Full Range of Leadership Development: Basic and Advanced Manuals*. Bass, Avolio & Associates.

Barnett, Gary, and Vahe Gregorian (2009). *High Hopes: Taking the Purple to Pasadena*. Hachette.

Bass, Bernard M. (1999). Two decades of research and development in transformational leadership. *European Journal of Work and Organizational Psychology*.

Bass, Bernard M., and Bruce J. Avolio (1994). *Improving Organizational Effectiveness Through Transformational Leadership*. Sage.

Bass, Bernard M., and Ronald E. Riggio (2006). *Transformational Leadership* (2nd ed.). Lawrence Erlbaum.

FIFA (2015, June 7). Norio Sasaki: We had to win after the disaster. YouTube. https://www.youtube.com/watch?v=savlOtPPrDQ.

Gonzales, Laurence (2004). *Deep Survival: Who Lives, Who Dies, and Why: True Stories of Miraculous Endurance and Sudden Death.* W.W. Norton.

Heiland, Teresa L., Robert Rovetti, and Jan Dunn (2012). Effects of visual, auditory, and kinesthetic imagery interventions on dancers' plié arabesques. *Journal of Imagery Research in Sport and Physical Activity.*

Jackson, Phil, and Hugh Delehanty (1995). *Sacred Hoops: Spiritual Lessons of a Hardwood Warrior.* Hyperion.

John Wooden (2020). Retrieved 20 November 2020, from https://en.wikipedia.org/wiki/John_Wooden.

Jowett, Sophia (2007). Interdependence analysis and the 3+1Cs in the coach-athlete relationship. In Sophia Jowett and David Lavallee (Eds.), *Social Psychology in Sport.* Human Kinetics.

Jowett, Sophia, and I.M. Cockerill (2003). Olympic medalists' perspective of the athlete–coach relationship. *Psychology of Sport and Exercise.*

Jowett, Sophia, and John Nezlek (2011). Relationship interdependence and satisfaction with important outcomes in coach-athlete dyads. *Journal of Social and Personal Relationships.*

Post, Phillip G., Craig A. Wrisberg, and Stephen Mullins (2010). A field test of the influence of pre-game imagery on basketball free throw shooting. *Journal of Imagery Research in Sport and Physical Activity.*

Robin, Nicolas, Laurent Dominique, Lucette Toussaint, Yannick Blandin, Aymeric Guillot, and Michel Le Her (2007). Effects of motor imagery training on service return accuracy in tennis: The role of imagery ability. *International Journal of Sport and Exercise Psychology.*

Rozin, Paul, and Edward B. Royzman (2001). Negativity bias, negativity dominance, and contagion. *Personality and Social Psychology Review.*

Vallée, Chantal N., and Gordon A. Bloom (2005). Building a successful university program: Key and common elements of expert coaches. *Journal of Applied Sport Psychology.*

Vallée, Chantal N., and Gordon A. Bloom (2016). Four keys to building a championship culture. *International Sport Coaching Journal.*

Wakefield, Caroline, and Dave Smith (2012). Perfecting practice: Applying the PETTLEP Model of motor imagery. *Journal of Sport Psychology in Action.*

Q2

Bandura, Albert, and Dale H. Schunk (1981). Cultivating competence, self-efficacy, and intrinsic interest through proximal self-motivation. *Journal of Personality and Social Psychology.*

Bloom, Gordon A., and Diane E. Stevens (2002). A team-building mental skills training program with an intercollegiate equestrian team. *Athletic Insight: The Online Journal of Sport Psychology.*

Bucci, Joseph, Gordon A. Bloom, Todd M. Loughead, and Jeffrey G. Caron (2012). Ice hockey coaches' perceptions of athlete leadership. *Journal of Applied Sport Psychology.*

Carron, Albert V., Michelle M. Colman, Jennifer Wheeler, and Diane Stevens (2002). Cohesion and performance in sport: A meta analysis. *Journal of Sport & Exercise Psychology.*

Cope, Cassandra J., Mark Eys, Mark Beauchamp, Robert Schinke, and Grégoire Bosselut (2011). Informal roles on sport teams. *International Journal of Sport & Exercise Psychology.*

Donoso-Morales, Daniela, Gordon A. Bloom, and Jeffrey G. Caron (2017). Creating and sustaining a culture of excellence: Insights from accomplished university team-sport coaches. *Research Quarterly for Exercise and Sport.*

Durand-Bush, Natalie, Jamie Collins, and Kylie McNeill (2012). Women coaches' experiences of stress and self-regulation: A multiple case study. *International Journal of Coaching Science.*

Dweck, Carol (2006). *Mindset: The New Psychology of Success.* Random House.

Ericsson, K. Anders, Ralf T. Krampe, and Clemens Tesch-Römer (1993). The role of deliberate practice in the acquisition of expert performance. *Psychological Review.*

Ericsson, K. Anders, Ralf T. Krampe, and Clemens Tesch-Römer (2019). Towards a science of the acquisition of expert performance in sports: Clarifying the differences between deliberate practice and other types of practice. *Journal of Sports Sciences.*

Filip (2013, November 28). Gregg Popovich on his first time meeting with Tim Duncan. YouTube. https://www.youtube.com/watch?v=QkKJh WoCehE.

Fraser, Madison M., Gordon A. Bloom, and Clifford J. Mallett (2024). University serial winning coaches' experiences with low performance and maladaptive team culture. *Psychology of Sport and Exercise.*

Gilbert, Wade (2017). *Coaching Better Every Season.* Human Kinetics.

Goleman, Daniel (1998). What makes a leader? *Harvard Business Review.*

Grant, Matthew A., Gordon A. Bloom, and Jordan S. Lefebvre (2020). Lessons learned: Coaches' perceptions of a pilot e-mentoring programme. *International Sport Coaching Journal.*

Heelis, William J., Jeffrey G. Caron, and Gordon A. Bloom (2020). The experiences of high-performance coaches in the management of difficult athletes. *Psychology of Sport and Exercise.*

Hodge, Ken, Graham Henry, and Wayne Smith (2014). A case study of excellence in elite sport: Motivational climate in a world champion team. *The Sport Psychologist.*

Kerr, James (2013). *Legacy: What the All Blacks Can Teach Us About the Business of Life.* Constable.

Kerr, Norbert L., Ann C. Rumble, Ernest S. Park, Jaap W. Ouwerkerk, Craig D. Parks, Marcello Gallucci, and Paul A.M. van Lange (2009). "How many bad apples does it take to spoil the whole barrel?": Social exclusion and toleration for bad apples. *Journal of Experimental Social Psychology.*

Kilty, Katie (2006). Women in coaching. *The Sport Psychologist.*

Kim, Jeemin, Gordon A. Bloom, and Andrew Bennie (2016). Intercollegiate coaches' experiences and strategies for coaching first-year athletes. *Qualitative Research in Sport, Exercise, and Health.*

Lefebvre, Jordan S., Gordon A. Bloom, and Todd M. Loughead (2020). A citation network analysis of career mentoring across disciplines: A roadmap for mentoring research in sport. *Psychology of Sport and Exercise.*

McCardle, Lindsay, Bradley W. Young, and Joseph Baker (2019). Self-regulated learning and expertise development in sport: Current status, challenges, and future opportunities. *International Review of Sport and Exercise Psychology.*

Milius, Inge, Wade Gilbert, Danielle Alexander, and Gordon A. Bloom (2021). Coaches' use of positive tactile communication in collegiate basketball. *International Sport Coaching Journal.*

NBA (2016, December 19). Tim Duncan's San Antonio Spurs Jersey Retirement (Full Ceremony). Retrieved from https://www.youtube.com/watch?v=WaZSfGTeqhQ.

Neely, Kacey C., John G.H. Dunn, Tara-Lee F. McHugh, and Nicholas Holt (2016). The deselection process in competitive female youth sport. *The Sport Psychologist*.

Paradis, Kyle, Albert V. Carron, and Luc J. Martin (2014). Athlete perceptions of intra-group conflict in sport teams. *Sport & Exercise Psychology Review*.

Urquhart, David A., Gordon A. Bloom, and Todd Loughead (2020). The development, articulation, and implementation of a coaching vision of multiple championship-winning university ice hockey coaches. *International Sport Coaching Journal*.

Q3

Billick, Brian (2001). *Developing an Offensive Gameplan*. Coaches Choice.

Bloom, Gordon A. (2013). Mentoring for sports coaches. In Paul Potrac, Wade Gilbert, and Jim Denison (Eds.), *The Routledge Handbook of Sports Coaching*. Routledge.

Bloom, Gordon A., Jordan S. Lefebvre, and Peter Smith (2018). Canadian case study conversation: Mentorship in elite women's ice hockey. In Fiona C. Chambers (Ed.), *Learning to Mentor in Sports Coaching: A Design Thinking Approach*. Routledge.

Clance, Pauline Rose, and Suzanne Imes (1978). The imposter phenomenon in high achieving women: Dynamics and therapeutic intervention. *Psychotherapy: Theory, Research & Practice*.

Côté, Jean, and Wade Gilbert (2009). An integrative definition of coaching effectiveness and expertise. *International Journal of Sports Science & Coaching*.

Davies, M.J., Gordon A. Bloom, and J.H. Salmela (2005). Job satisfaction of accomplished male university basketball coaches: The Canadian context. *International Journal of Sport Psychology*.

Donoso-Morales, Daniela, Gordon A. Bloom, and Jeffrey G. Caron (2017). Creating and sustaining a culture of excellence: Insights from accomplished university team-sport coaches. *Research Quarterly for Exercise and Sport.*

Eby, Lillian T., Jean E. Rhodes, and Tammy D. Allen (2007). Definition and evolution of mentoring. In Tammy D. Allen and Lillian T. Eby (Eds.), *The Blackwell Handbook of Mentoring: A Multiple Perspectives Approach.* Blackwell.

Florence Chadwick. (2020). Retrieved 20 November 2020, from https://en.wikipedia.org/wiki/Florence_Chadwick.

Ghorbanshirodi, Shohreh (2012). The relationship between self-esteem and emotional intelligence with imposter syndrome among medical students of Guilan and Heratsi Universities. *Journal of Basic and Applied Scientific Research.*

Jones, Robyn L., Richard Harris, and Andrew Miles (2009). Mentoring in sports coaching: A review of literature. *Physical Education and Sport Pedagogy.*

Knowles, Zoe, David Gilbourne, Andy Borrie, and Alan Michael Nevill (2001). Developing the reflective sports coach: A study exploring the processes of reflective practice within a higher education coaching programme. *Reflective Practice.*

Knowles, Zoe, David Gilbourne, Brendan Cropley, and Lindsey Dugdill (2014). Reflecting on reflection and journeys. In Zoe Knowles and Brendan Cropley (Eds.), *Reflective Practice in the Sport and Exercise Science: Contemporary Issues.* Routledge.

Kunich, John C., and Richard L. Lester (1999). Leadership and the art of mentoring: Tool kit for the time machine. *Journal of Leadership and Organizational Studies.*

Lara-Bercial, Sergio, and Cliff Mallett (2016). The practices and developmental pathways of professional and Olympic serial winning coaches. *International Sport Coaching Journal.*

Lashinsky, Adam (2012). *Inside Apple: How America's Most Admired—and Secretive—Company Really Works.* Business Plus HBG.

Lefebvre, Jordan S., Gordon A. Bloom, and Lindsay R. Duncan (2021). A qualitative examination of the developmental networks of elite sport coaches. *Sport, Exercise, and Performance Psychology.*

Mallett, Clifford J., and Sergio Lara-Bercial (2016). Serial winning coaches: People, vision, and environment. In Markus Raab,

Paul Wylleman, Roland Seiler, Anne-Marie Elbe, and Antonis Hatzigeorgiadis (Eds.), *Sport and Exercise Psychology Research: From Theory to Practice*. Elsevier.

McKimm, Judy, Carol Jollie, and Mark Hatter (2007). Mentoring: Theory and practice. *London Deanery Faculty Development*.

Nater, Swen, and Ronald Gallimore (2010). *You Haven't Taught Until They Have Learned: John Wooden's Teaching Principles and Practices*. Fitness Information Technology.

Rathwell, Scott, Gordon A. Bloom, and Todd Loughead (2014). Head coaches' perceptions on the roles, selection and development of the assistant coach. *International Sport Coaching Journal*.

Sinotte, Charles-Antoine, Gordon A. Bloom, and Jeffrey G. Caron (2015). Roles, responsibilities, and relationships of full-time university assistant coaches. *Sports Coaching Review*.

Snyder, C. (2011, January). Leadership thought: How to handle an assistant coach. *Lacrosse Magazine*.

Solomon, G.B. (2001). Performance and personality expectations of assistant coaches: Implications for athlete performance. *International Sports Journal*.

Urquhart, David A., Gordon A. Bloom, and Todd Loughead (2020). The development, articulation, and implementation of a coaching vision of multiple championship-winning university ice hockey coaches. *International Sport Coaching Journal*.

Vallée, Chantal N., and Gordon A. Bloom (2005). Building a successful university sport program: Key and common elements of expert coaches. *Journal of Applied Sport Psychology*.

Villwock, Jennifer A., Lindsay B. Sobin, Lindsey A. Koester, and Tucker M. Harris (2016). Imposter syndrome and burnout among American medical students: A pilot study. *International Journal of Medical Education*.

Walt Disney. (2020). Retrieved 20 November 2020, from https://www.biography.com/business-figure/walt-disney.

Wiman, Melissa, Alan W. Salmoni, and Craig R. Hall (2010). An examination of the definition and development of expert coaching. *International Journal of Coaching Science*.

Young, Valeria (2011). *The Secret Thoughts of Successful Women: Why Capable People Suffer from the Impostor Syndrome and How to Thrive in Spite of It.* Crown Business.

Q4

Ashton-Shaeffer, Candace, Heather Gibson, Marieke Holt, and Cynthia Willming (2001). Women's resistance and empowerment through wheelchair sport. *World Leisure Journal.*

Beaumont, Chris, Ian W. Maynard, and Joanne Butt (2015). Effective ways to develop and maintain robust sport-confidence: Strategies advocated by sport psychology consultants. *Journal of Applied Sport Psychology.*

Blinde, Elaine M., Diane E. Taub, and Lingling Han (1994). Sport as a site for women's group and societal empowerment: Perspectives from the college athlete. *Sociology of Sport Journal.*

Camiré, Martin, Pierre Trudel, and Tanya Forneris (2012). Coaching and transferring life skills: Philosophies and strategies used by model high school coaches. *The Sport Psychologist.*

Csikszentmihalyi, Mihaly, Kevin Rathunde, and Samuel Whalen (1993). *Talented Teenagers: The Roots of Success and Failure.* Cambridge University Press.

Duckworth, Angela (2016). *Grit: The Power of Passion and Perseverance.* Scribner / Simon & Schuster.

Dundjerski, Marina (2011). *UCLA: The First Century.* Third Millenium.

Falcão, William, Gordon A. Bloom, and Andrew Bennie (2017). Coaches' experiences learning and applying the content of a humanistic coaching workshop in youth sport settings. *International Sport Coaching Journal.*

Falcão, William, Gordon A. Bloom, and Catherine M. Sabiston (2020). The impact of humanistic coach training on youth athletes' development through sport. *International Journal of Sports Science & Coaching.*

Fletcher, David, and Mustafa Sarkar (2016). Mental fortitude training: An evidence-based approach to developing psychological resilience for sustained success. *Journal of Sport Psychology in Action.*

Gilbert, Wade (2010). The passing of a legend: Coach John Wooden. *International Journal of Sports Science & Coaching.*

Gould, Daniel, and Sarah Carson (2008). Life skills development through sport: Current status and future directions. *International Review of Sport and Exercise Psychology.*

Gould, Daniel, Sarah Carson, Angela Fifer, Larry Lauer, and Robert Benham (2009). Stakeholders' perceptions of social-emotional and life skill development issues characterizing contemporary high school sports. *Journal of Coaching Education.*

Goyens, Chris, and Allan Turowetz (1986). *Lions in Winter.* Prentice Hall.

Hays, Kate, Owen Thomas, Ian Maynard, and Mark Bawden (2009). The role of confidence in world-class sport performance. *Journal of Sports Sciences.*

Horrell, Sara, Hazel Johnson, and Paul Mosley (Eds.) (2008). *Work, Female Empowerment and Economic Development.* Routledge.

Jowett, Sophia (2007). Interdependence analysis and the 3+1Cs in the coach-athlete relationship. In Sophia Jowett and David Lavallee (Eds.), *Social Psychology in Sport.* Human Kinetics.

Lara-Bercial, Sergio, and Clifford J. Mallett (2016). The practices and developmental pathways of professional and Olympic serial winning coaches. *International Sport Coaching Journal.*

Liechty, Toni, Fleesha Willfong, and Katie Sveinson (2016). Embodied experiences of empowerment among female tackle football players. *Sociology of Sport Journal.*

Loughead, Todd, and Gordon A. Bloom (2016). Coach and athlete leadership in sport. In Robert J. Schinke, Kerry R. McGannon, and Brett Smith (Eds.), *Routledge International Handbook of Sport Psychology.* Routledge.

Lombardo, Bennett J. (1987). *The Humanistic Coach: From Theory to Practice.* Charles C. Thomas.

Lyle, John (2002). *Sports Coaching Concepts: A Framework for Coaches' Behaviour.* Routledge.

Machida, Moe, Mark Otten, T. Michelle Magyar, Robin S. Vealey, and Rose Marie Ward (2017). Examining multidimensional sport-confidence in athletes and non-athlete sport performers. *Journal of Sports Sciences.*

Malik, Samina, and Kathy Courtney (2011). Higher education and women's empowerment in Pakistan. *Gender and Education*.

Mehta, Pallavi, and Khushboo Sharma (2014). Leadership: Determinant of women empowerment. *SCMS Journal of Indian Management*.

Moghadam, Valentine M. (2010). Gender, politics, and women's empowerment. In Kevin T. Leicht and J. Craig Jenkins (Eds.), *Handbook of Politics*. Springer.

SUCCESS Academy (Producer) (2016). *Coach: The Life and Legacy of John R. Wooden*. [Documentary Short]. Retrieved from https://www .thewoodeneffect.com/.

Velija, Philippa, Mark Mierzwinski, and Laura Fortune (2013). 'It made me feel powerful': Women's gendered embodiment and physical empowerment in the martial arts. *Leisure Studies*.

OVERTIME

Alexander, Danielle, Gordon A. Bloom, and Shaunna L. Taylor (2020). Female Paralympic athlete views on effective and ineffective coaching practices. *Journal of Applied Sport Psychology*.

Banwell, Jenessa, Gretchen Kerr, and Ashley Stirling (2021). Benefits of a female coach mentorship programme on women coaches' development: An ecological perspective. *Sports Coaching Review*.

Banwell, Jenessa, Gretchen Kerr, and Ashley Stirling (2019). Key considerations for advancing women in coaching. *Women in Sport and Physical Activity Journal*.

Chang, Jihyun, Pyounggu Baek, and Taesung Kim (2021). Women's developmental networks and career satisfaction: Developmental functions as a mediator. *Journal of Career Development*.

Cope, Cassandra J., Mark Eys, Mark Beauchamp, Robert Schinke, and Grégoire Bosselut (2010). Coaches' perspectives of a negative informal role: The 'cancer' within sport teams. *Journal of Applied Sport Psychology*.

Culver, Diane, Erin Kraft, Cari Din, and Isabelle Cayer (2019). The Alberta women in sport leadership project: A social learning intervention for gender equity and leadership development. *Women in Sport and Physical Activity Journal*.

Frontiera, Joe (2010). Leadership and organizational culture transformation in professional sport. *Journal of Leadership & Organizational Studies*.

Giacobbi, Peter R., Joe Whitney, Emily Roper, and Ted Butryn (2002). College coaches' views about the development of successful athletes: A descriptive exploratory investigation. *Journal of Sport Behavior*.

Gould, Daniel, Kristen Dieffenbach, and Aaron Moffett (2002). Psychological characteristics and their development in Olympic champions. *Journal of Applied Sport Psychology*.

Heelis, William J., Jeffrey G. Caron, and Gordon A. Bloom (2020). The experiences of high-performance coaches in the management of difficult athletes. *Psychology of Sport and Exercise*.

Holley, Michael (2011). *War Room: The Legacy of Bill Belichick and the Art of Building the Perfect Team*. HarperCollins.

Kilty, Katie (2006). Women in coaching. *The Sport Psychologist*.

Kotter, John P., and James L. Heskett (2008). *Corporate Culture and Performance*. Simon & Schuster.

LaVoi, Nicole, and Julia K. Dutove (2012). Barriers and supports for female coaches: An ecological model. *Sports Coaching Review*.

Leggat, Fiona J., Matthew J. Smith, and Sean G. Figgins (2020). Talented but disruptive: An exploration of problematic players in sports teams. *Journal of Applied Sport Psychology*.

Neely, Kacey C., John G.H. Dunn, Tara-Lee F. McHugh, and Nicholas Holt (2016). The deselection process in competitive female youth sport. *The Sport Psychologist*.

Oterino, Ivan (2015). Great GMs are made, not born. Retrieved from https://www.kornferry.com/insights/this-week-in-leadership/great-gms-are-made-not-born.

Rathwell, Scott, Gordon A. Bloom, and Todd Loughead (2014). Head coaches' perceptions on the roles, selection and development of the assistant coach. *International Sport Coaching Journal*.

Wachsmuth, Svenja, Sophia Jowett, and Chris G. Harwood (2018). Managing conflict in coach-athlete relationships. *Sport, Exercise, and Performance Psychology*.

Wachsmuth, Svenja, Sophia Jowett, and Chris G. Harwood (2018). On understanding the nature of interpersonal conflicts between coaches and athletes. *Journal of Sport Sciences.*

Williams Madeleine (2013). A pragmatic solution for gender equity in Canadian elite sport. *International Sports Law Journal.*

ACKNOWLEDGMENTS

CHANTAL

I would like to thank everyone who has contributed to *Dare to Win*, including those who provided endorsements, feedback, and countless hours of editing: Vanessa H., Sylvia J., Valerie B., Jenny M., Kris H., Lucas R., Don M., Tom F., Madeline B., Helene B., Ghislain P., Marty G., Dan W., Sharon P., Michael H., and the entire team at ECW Press.

To my many athletes, assistant coaches, mentors, colleagues, student staff (past and present), my family, and all supporters in the Windsor community. Thank you for helping bring this vision to life.

GORDON

I would like to give special thanks to my family for allowing me to pursue my dreams in sport psychology. Additionally, thanks to my research collaborators and current and former graduate students who have all played a part in this amazing career of mine, by providing continuous coaching, support, and encouragement.

ABOUT THE AUTHORS

COACH CHANTAL VALLÉE is the current head coach of the University of Windsor women's basketball team, a program that went from the bottom of the rankings in Canada to a record five consecutive national championships. She has also made history as the first woman to simultaneously hold the positions of head coach and general manager of a men's professional team, the Hamilton Honey Badgers, which reached the championship final under her leadership in the franchise's first professional season. Chantal's success stems from her application of her own published scientific findings as a researcher of leadership and coaching success. Her proven theory-to-practice methods helps distinguish her from others. Recognized for her expertise, she is frequently sought after as a consultant by both Canadian and American corporations. Chantal is also an accomplished author, having attained Amazon bestseller status. To learn more about her remarkable journey, visit her website at CoachVallee.com.

DR. GORDON BLOOM is a professor and director of the Sport Psychology Research Laboratory (https://www.mcgill.ca/sportpsych) in the Department of Kinesiology and Physical Education at the prestigious McGill University. Gordon has developed an internationally recognized coaching research program related to the knowledge, strategies, and behaviours employed by coaches in terms of leadership practices, mentoring, and team building that develop successful teams and athletes. He has incorporated the findings of his research in his role as a mental performance consultant with amateur, professional, Olympic, and Paralympic athletes and teams. He has also received numerous invitations from academic and sport coaching associations around the globe to present his research and practical experiences to scientists, athletes, administrators, and coaches. Dr. Bloom still enjoys competing in ice hockey, ball hockey, tennis, and softball and coaching youth sport.